Kapitza, Rutherford, and the Kremlin

KAPITZA, RUTHERFORD, AND THE KREMLIN

Lawrence Badash

Yale University Press
New Haven and London

Designed by Nancy Ovedovitz and set in Galliard type by East-
ern Graphics. Printed in the United States of America by Book-
Crafters, Inc., Chelsea, Michigan.

Library of Congress Cataloging in Publication Data

Badash, Lawrence.
    Kapitza, Rutherford, and the Kremlin.
    Includes index.
    1. Kapifsa, P. L. (Petr Leonidovich), 1894–1984. 2. Science
and state–Soviet Union. 3. Rutherford, Ernest, 1871–1937.
4. Physicists—Biography. I. Title.
QC16.K25B3 1985   530'.092'2   84-11822
ISBN 0-300-01465-1

The paper in this book meets the guidelines for permanence and
durability of the Committee on Production Guidelines for Book
Longevity of the Council on Library Resources.

10 9 8 7 6 5 4 3 2 1

To the memories of
Ernest Rutherford (1871 – 1937)
and
Peter Kapitza (1894 – 1984)

⟪ Contents ⟫

⫷ Preface ⫸

It is impossible today to escape the realization that we live in a scientific age. Whether the news is frightening, as about nuclear, chemical, or biological weapons, or pleasing, as the cure for some dread disease, or just curious, as the fact that most of the scientists who ever lived are alive today, we find ourselves increasingly affected by the results of scientific research. It was not always so; this pervasive social impact of science is a twentieth century phenomenon. The transition from the "little science" of past years to the "Big Science" we now encounter came about through the transfusion of considerable amounts of money into the profession. As physicists sought to study smaller and smaller pieces of matter, they needed larger and more expensive pieces of apparatus. And as governments learned that pure research could lead to significant scientific devices, such as atomic bombs, their treasuries were opened to those with the appropriate technical credentials.

Peter Kapitza was a major figure in this transition, on both levels. First, he was a physicist with engineering talents who devised and had constructed large machines for his particular investigations. His ability to extract the necessary funds from his patron, Rutherford, was considered phenomenal by others in the Cavendish Laboratory. Then, he became caught in the growing pains of Soviet science, when his government insisted on planning this activity but had little idea how to do so. His forced involvement is a classic example of the relations between science and government before they came to understand each other.

Kapitza's death in April 1984, long after this transitional generation flourished, beckons us to reflect upon our "progress." We have come a long way since the mid-1930s, when the events described in this book occurred. Great numbers of scientists now serve government, as consultants or in government agencies and laboratories, while tax revenues fund a variety of institutions, research projects, fellowships, and so on. But this more intimate and mutually beneficial relationship does not mean that there are no problems. Indeed, some of the very issues raised in connection with Kapitza still linger. Is science international? Can science progress properly under a totalitarian regime? (The question used to be, Can it progress at all?) Have scientists an obligation to look for applications of their knowledge which may benefit mankind, or at least their countrymen? Or, conversely, have they an obligation to refrain from activities which they see as socially irresponsible? Can scientific discovery be planned, as one would a factory for producing automobiles? Much thought and discussion have attended such questions, producing enlightenment if not resolution. Yet this is a historical work, seeking to answer the "how" and "why" of Kapitza's troubles, and to place them in a larger context, not a study in the sociology of science. Thus I mention such themes in this preface, to sensitize the reader to their appearance, but do not pursue them in the text.

I have made extensive use of the unpublished Rutherford materials in the University Library, Cambridge, England, whose officials I wish to thank for their help. This collection is physically in two sections: correspondence and papers. Unless specified in my notes as from the Rutherford correspondence or other sources, all references are to materials in the Rutherford papers. I am indebted also to many British scientists, friends and colleagues of Rutherford and Kapitza, for their views on the subject of this book, and also to the Center for the History of Physics of the American Institute of Physics. This material is based upon work supported by the National Science Foundation under grant GS-2618.

I wish to thank Alexander Metro for his skill and high standard of craftsmanship in seeing this book through publication.

There is at least one convention for the English spelling of Russian names, but I have chosen to follow no set of rules. Though the lack of consistency will bring tears to the eyes of Russian scholars, I have used the spelling commonly given in England in the 1930s, in Kapitza's letters, and in reference works I have considered appropriate.

During the first year of his detention in Russia Kapitza wrote numerous letters to his wife, Anna, then in England. From about one-quarter of the total she excerpted portions for Rutherford's use. The extra spaces within letters represent material Anna has omitted. These, and the few other Kapitza letters that appear in this volume, have been minimally edited. Spelling has been corrected, some punctuation has been supplied, and a few extraneous words have been deleted. But grammar and word usage have not been touched, and the charm of Kapitza's prose remains intact.

⋘ Introduction ⋙

It was the twentieth anniversary of the ill-fated troop landings at Gallipoli, yet British newspaper headlines called attention to present, not past, world difficulties. "CAMBRIDGE HAS SHOCK FROM THE SOVIET; FAMOUS SCIENTIST RECALLED," ran the banner in the *News Chronicle* of 24 April 1935. "RUSSIA TO KEEP HIM; HALT TO CAMBRIDGE STUDIES," echoed the *Star*. Over the next few days it became clear that not the letter, but the spirit, of international law was being tested in a case of unique circumstances.

Although Peter Kapitza had studied and worked in England for thirteen years, had been elected a Fellow of Trinity College and of the Royal Society, had received thousands of pounds of research support from the British government and other sources, had been appointed to one of the Royal Society's research professorships, and had just had a £15,000 laboratory built for him by the Royal Society, he nevertheless retained his Russian citizenship. On a summer visit to his homeland in 1934, he had been told firmly that the Soviet government desired his services and that he could not leave the country. No one could argue that the Russians lacked the legal right to their action, but the world scientific community, which liked to feel that its pursuits transcended national boundaries, was shocked by the brutal interruption of Kapitza's work and the Soviet ingratitude for Britain's exceedingly generous support over the years.

Even more seriously, those few close associates in Cambridge who remained in contact with Kapitza during the first year of his "captivity" were aware that his growing frustration was leading him perilously close to a mental breakdown. Because he was a sensitive man whose work progressed smoothly in tranquil surroundings, it was

1

feared that the agonies of his repeated but unproductive encounters with the Soviet bureaucracy, and his reluctance to assume charge of the laboratory his government wished to build for him, might render him permanently incapable of scientific work.

The story of Kapitza's detention in his own country is one of personal tragedy—with an added twist. Although not a Communist party member, he was a loyal son of Russia who recognized the urgent need to modernize the economy and improve social conditions as much in one generation as had taken countries of the West centuries. That this would involve hardships, dislocations, and widespread suffering was accepted as unavoidable for the greater good of the motherland. Thus, Kapitza, who felt that the treatment he had received was counterproductive, was caught up in the logic of a system he supported.

His story is also one of science and government in the days before these two forces had much contact. True, princes of old supported alchemists and patronized other branches of science; some governments aided scientific pursuits connected with navigation, exploration, public health, and economic geology; and the value of national bureaus of standards was recognized, but in general contact and understanding between scientists and bureaucrats were slight. This is perhaps symbolized by the apocryphal story that, upon entry of the United States into World War I, officials of the American Chemical Society called the War Department to offer the services of their membership and were thanked politely but told, "We already have a chemist."[1] Even in a society such as Soviet Russia's, where "scientific" plans were laid to promote rapid progress, such orientation was mostly toward technology, which could help far more than science in industrialization.

To a very large degree, science was first seen by governments to be of fundamental importance during World War II. And the irony, as seen by some pure scientists, is that this recognition was based upon applied science. Yet, such products as the atomic bomb and radar have convinced nations that science is too valuable to be ignored;

1. This story is told by James B. Conant, *Modern Science and Modern Man* (Garden City, N.Y.: Doubleday Anchor, 1953), pp. 18–19.

rather, to a large extent it must be controlled. Kapitza's plight, then, may be seen as a significant step along the path of greater mutual influence between science and government.

««« 1 »»»

Kapitza in Cambridge

When Kapitza began work in Cambridge's world-famous Cavendish Laboratory in 1921, its director, Sir Ernest Rutherford, bluntly told him that communist propaganda would not be tolerated. Rutherford, single-minded in his devotion to scientific research and essentially apolitical, was suspicious of anyone from Russia so soon after the Revolution. Kapitza said nothing, but the painful encounter remained long in his memory. When, the following year, he published a paper on the loss of energy of an alpha-ray beam in its passage through matter, the inscription on the reprint he handed to Rutherford pointed out that he had indeed come to England to do scientific work and not make political propaganda. Rutherford's enormous temper flared, whereupon Kapitza produced from behind his back another copy of his paper bearing a more conventional inscription. This Rutherford accepted, appreciating Kapitza's foresight, and the incident was buried under the warm friendship which followed.[1] So highly, in fact, did Rutherford regard the young Russian's abilities and so attractive did he find Kapitza's mercurial personality, that the latter was widely considered the professor's favorite out of an extremely distinguished group of pupils Rutherford had over the years.

Pyotr Leonidovich Kapitza was born in Kronstadt on 8 July 1894 and received his early education in that city. He then went to nearby Petrograd (formerly St. Petersburg, now Leningrad) for training as an electrical engineer in the Polytechnic Institute, perhaps with the goal of following in the footsteps of his father, a general in the czar's

1. P. L. Kapitza, "Recollections of Lord Rutherford," *Proceedings of the Royal Society*, A294 (1966), 131.

engineer corps. By the time of his graduation in 1918, however, the Revolution would have foreclosed such plans and Kapitza remained at the institute as a lecturer until 1921. During these years he came under the influence of Abram Joffé, one of Russia's outstanding physicists and a man who had been a pupil of Röntgen, the discoverer of x rays. With his mind turned increasingly toward science, Kapitza was regarded as a young man with great promise. But tragedy now struck in the form of an influenza epidemic which carried off his wife and two children. In an effort to shake him from his deep grief, friends suggested him for an official trade-scientific mission abroad. This group, which included Joffé and whose director was the noted naval architect, engineer, and mathematician Aleksei Krylov, was to reestablish scientific contacts in Western Europe and to purchase scientific instruments, supplies, and machine shop equipment.[2] An ulterior purpose was to explain to foreign scholars the scientific policy of the new Soviet system.[3]

The others reached their first destination in Germany but Kapitza got only as far as Estonia. Germany refused him a visa, claiming he was a potential agitator among the young; France and Holland did likewise. This enforced idleness on the shores of the Baltic lasted several months, during which time Kapitza decided that he would like to seek scientific opportunities greater than those available in his homeland. Characteristically, he set his sights high and applied to Cambridge University's Cavendish Laboratory. The details of his acceptance are uncertain, but he was granted a visa and arrived in England in the summer of 1921.[4]

2. Biographical information has been obtained from such standard sources as *Who's Who, Who's Who in Soviet Science, Who's Who in USSR,* and *Soviet Men of Science.* Also, D. Danin, *Rutherford* (in Russian; Moscow: Young Guard Publishing House, 1966). Kapitza read the manuscript of Danin's book, so presumably the information it gives about him is accurate.

3. O. M. Karpenko, G. V. Knyazev, A. V. Kol'tsov, S. G. Korneyev, Ye. S. Likhtenshteyn, and A. I. Shirokova, *The Academy of Sciences of the USSR, A Brief Account of Its History and Work* (English translation distributed by Clearinghouse, U.S. Department of Commerce, 1969), p. 99.

4. A charming anecdote about Kapitza's arrival in Cambridge still circulates in that university town. According to this story, Rutherford refused to admit Kapitza because the laboratory already was seriously overcrowded. Impetuously, the young Russian asked the great physicist, "How many research students have you?" "About

Peter Kapitza (about 1925). Courtesy of Peter Kapitza.

Cambridge at this time was the world center for experimental radioactivity, atomic physics, and nuclear physics. Indeed, it would be more precise to say that *Rutherford* was the center of such studies. Born in New Zealand in 1871, this hearty farmer's son had scaled the heights of physical science. Trained first in the antipodes and then in the Cavendish Laboratory under J. J. Thomson, he succes-

---

thirty," was the reply. "What is the customary accuracy of your experiments?" was the next question, to which Rutherford replied, "About two or three percent." "Well then," Kapitza beamed, "one more student would not even be noticed within that accuracy!" On the other hand, Albert Parry, ed., *Peter Kapitsa on Life and Science* (New York: Macmillan, 1968), p. 4, notes that Kapitza's reputation had preceded him and Rutherford at once made a place for him. There is some reason to believe that Kapitza was recommended by a former student of Rutherford, which would indeed have helped his case, but I do not share Parry's belief in the extent and efficacy of Kapitza's reputation at that time. Parry and I also differ on some other details of Kapitza's life

Ernest Rutherford (1932). Courtesy of the Cambridge University Library.

sively held professorships at McGill University in Montreal (1898–1907), Manchester University (1907–19), and Cambridge University (1919–37). Numerous honors came to him during his active career, including the Nobel Prize in 1908, knighthood in 1914, the Order of Merit in 1925, presidency of the Royal Society from 1925 to 1930, and a peerage as Baron Rutherford in 1931.[5]

---

and career. His sources are mostly published articles and communications from some émigrés. My sources are mostly unpublished documents from the Rutherford collection and personal interviews with several dozen of Rutherford's pupils. While our disagreements do not change the story in any fundamental way, it is understandable that I believe my version is more correct.

5. For biographical information see L. Badash, "Ernest Rutherford," *Dictionary of Scientific Biography;* A. S. Eve, *Rutherford* (Cambridge: University Press, 1939); N. Feather, *Lord Rutherford* (London: Blackie, 1940); E. N. da C. Andrade, *Rutherford and the Nature of the Atom* (Garden City, N.Y.: Doubleday, 1964).

Whereas most famous scientists are remembered for a single significant discovery, Rutherford may be credited with at least three major contributions. When the century was but a few years old he and Frederick Soddy advanced their transformation theory of radioactivity: radioactive atoms were spontaneously disintegrating, forming different "daughter" atoms in the process. This was an iconoclastic thought for those who considered atoms to be eternally unchangeable. A decade before Kapitza's arrival at the Cavendish Rutherford showed that the atom is not a solid, homogeneous mass, with lumps (electrons) scattered throughout it, but actually consists mostly of empty space with an extremely dense and tiny nucleus at the center and electrons moving about in the remainder of the atomic volume. Gone were the "billiard ball" and the "plum pudding" atomic models; in their place was the nuclear atom. This was the beginning of modern ideas of atomic structure. And finally, in the year that he left Manchester to succeed his own teacher, J. J. Thomson, as head of the premier physics laboratory in the world, Rutherford revealed that when alpha particles from radioactive materials were allowed to bombard certain elements there resulted transmutations into other elements. Since such changes clearly involved an alteration of the atom's nucleus, Rutherford's work set the stage for investigations of nuclear structure.

Such were to be the major pursuits in the Cavendish Laboratory during the 1920s and 1930s, and such was the scene Kapitza entered in 1921. Like all new research students, he was presumably given a quick course in radioactivity and then assigned a topic to investigate by the director or by one of the more senior men such as James Chadwick or C. D. Ellis. The particles emitted by radioactive nuclei were thought to be constituents of these nuclei, so study of their properties was a major means of gaining information about nuclear structure. A widely used tool for observing the alpha and beta particle tracks was the cloud chamber perfected by C. T. R. Wilson just before World War I. Kapitza employed this device in conjunction with a magnet which bent the paths of the charged particles, and three of his first four published papers dealt with such problems.

By 1924, however, the electrical engineer in him became more interested in the magnets he was using than in the application of this apparatus. Magnetic fields of great intensity were difficult to produce because of the large electrical supply required and the great amounts of heat generated. Kapitza reasoned that many experimental purposes could be served by a magnetic field lasting a fraction of a second, instead of the customary steady field, and that properly constructed apparatus need not suffer structural damage when the large electrical current is discharged through the electromagnet's coils in a short time. Over the next several years he succeeded in perfecting this technique, achieving increasingly higher fields and using them to examine the properties of materials under these unusual conditions.

That Rutherford permitted the large expenditures necessary for such equipment is a measure of his belief in Kapitza. The "Prof." had made his greatest discoveries with simple bits of homemade and hand-size apparatus. Economy and simplicity of experiment were his hallmarks. Yet Rutherford's genius in this regard was but the crowning glory of a very solid Cavendish tradition, the "sealing wax and string" approach to physics. Essentially, this meant the use of the cheapest and least durable materials suitable for a given experiment, and stories about the enforcement of this "rule" by the laboratory steward are legion. Kapitza's engineering skill, however, seems to have fascinated Rutherford; here was a man who made mechanical drawings for the machine shop operators when he needed special apparatus constructed! Then, too, Kapitza required electrical equipment that could more easily, and perhaps also less expensively, be made by industry. So Rutherford could justify to himself Kapitza's relatively large budget.

It is possible also that Rutherford backed Kapitza because he anticipated certain results from the young Russian's work that never materialized. Since the time he first transmuted an atom deliberately, Rutherford recognized that he was limited by the number and energy of his alpha particle "bullets," which came from naturally decaying radioactive substances. If he could obtain a greater supply of projectiles and a means to accelerate them, he would be able to effect more transmutations in more elements. The obvious mechanism was to pull the charged particles across a large potential, but the technology to achieve the necessary hundreds of thousands or millions of volts had not yet been developed. Indeed, it was not until the early 1930s that Cockcroft and Walton, in the Cavendish Laboratory, and

Peter Kapitza (about 1930). Courtesy of Peter Kapitza.

Van de Graaff, in America, succeeded in building such generators, only to have them superseded in widespread usage by Lawrence's cyclotron. The cyclotron sidesteps the need for unusually high voltages by imparting a series of smaller "kicks," or energy increments, to the charged particles as they spiral inside the accelerator.

Precisely this idea of cumulative effects was current in the previous decade and may have influenced Rutherford's willingness to support Kapitza. As early as 1920, S. Evershed had suggested the possibility of disturbing the electronic orbits within atoms of a magnetic substance by imposing upon them intense magnetic fields.[6] Calculation showed, however, that even with fields many times stronger than

6. S. Evershed, "Permanent magnets in theory and practice," *Journal of the Institution of Electrical Engineers,* 58 (1920), 835. In a review of E. C. Stoner's *Magnetism and Atomic Structure,* in *Nature,* 119 (4 June 1927), 809–10, Kapitza wrote: "The

Ernest Rutherford (about 1932). Courtesy of the Royal Institution, London.

those normally attainable, the change in the magnetic moment of a revolving electron would be only of the order of one-tenth of 1 percent. T. F. Wall, at Sheffield University, then advanced the thought that repeated application of the field might cause increasing stress on the atom, making the effect more noticeable.[7] Wall worked on de-

---

magnetic field is probably the only practical weapon by means of which we may hope to change the motion and arrangement of the electrons in the atom, and thus influence all the physical and chemical properties of the atom. In only a very few cases at the present time do we find that the influence of the magnetic field on the properties of the atom is noticed. This is because the influence of the available fields is too weak. . . ."

7. T. F. Wall, "The generation of very intense magnetic fields," *Journal of the Institution of Electrical Engineers,* 64 (1926), 745–57.

Physics staff and research students, June 1932. *Third row standing:* N. S. Alexander, P. Wright, A. G. Hill, J. L. Pawsey, G. Occhialini, H. Miller; *second row standing:* W. E. Duncanson, E. C. Childs, T. G. P. Tarrant, J. McDougall, R. C. Evans, E. S. Shire, E. L. C. White, F. H. Nicoll, R. M. Chaudhri, B. V. Bowden, W. B. Lewis, *first row standing:* P. C. Ho, C. B. Mohr, H. W. S. Massey, M. L. Oliphant, E. T. S. Walton, C. E. Wynn-Williams, J. K. Roberts, N. Feather, Miss Davies, Miss Sparshott, J. P. Gott; *seated:* J. A. Ratcliffe, P. Kapitza, J. Chadwick, R. Ladenberg, Prof. Sir J. J. Thomson, Prof. Lord Rutherford, Prof. C. T. R. Wilson, F. W. Aston, C. D. Ellis, P. M. S. Blackett, J. D. Cockcroft. Courtesy of the Cavendish Laboratory, Cambridge University.

vices for the generation of high magnetic fields, and Kapitza was familiar with his approach, but nothing more about disrupting atoms magnetically seems to have been forthcoming. Probably Rutherford had doubts that such stresses on an atom's orbital electrons could lead to fragmentation of the nucleus, but he was inclined often to try any "damn-fool experiment" on the off-chance that it might work.

On the basis of his work in radioactivity, Kapitza, who was en-rolled as a student in Trinity College working toward his doctoral degree, was awarded the Clerk Maxwell Studentship in 1923 by the university and retained it for three years. His subsequent work with magnetic fields was equally appreciated, and in 1925 he was elected a Fellow of Trinity, the most famous of the many colleges comprising Cambridge University and the college of which Rutherford was a se-nior Fellow and J. J. Thomson the Master.

Rutherford's pervasive influence was effective on another front also, for in 1924 he obtained from the government's Department of Scientific and Industrial Research (DSIR) a grant to purchase equip-ment for a magnetic research laboratory within the Cavendish. Ka-pitza, for whom this was established, was appointed Assistant Direc-tor of Magnetic Research by the university, Rutherford being the tit-ular director. In March 1926 the new laboratory was formally

Peter Kapitza and electrical generator for experiments with high magnetic fields. Courtesy of the Cambridge University Library.

Royal Society Mond Laboratory, Cambridge University.

opened by the university's chancellor, Lord Balfour. By the summer of 1930 the DSIR had provided more than £16,000 to cover equipment, salaries, and running expenses,[8] an amount considerably larger than that which was spent upon the *primary* research pursuits of the Cavendish. But Kapitza could rightly claim that his apparatus cost far more than the cloud chambers, electrometers, electroscopes, and Geiger counters commonly used by the atomic physicists in these days just before the birth of "atom smashing" machines.

While he professed to despise administrative work, Kapitza nevertheless became thoroughly involved in it. In 1928, a Department of Magnetic Research was created as a subdepartment of the Physics Department, with Kapitza as its effective head. By this time he began to see that a desirable extension of his work would require the examination of materials under high magnetic fields *and* very low tempera-

8. "History and constitution of the Department of Magnetic Research," a five-page typed outline, prepared about 1931.

tures, when matter generally behaves quite differently than at ordinary temperatures. Consequently, a liquid hydrogen plant was erected for the attainment of these conditions.

Yet by early 1930 Kapitza felt frustrated.[9] In his early efforts he had achieved magnetic fields of 100,000 gauss, substantially higher than others had reached, and had shown that they were experimentally useful during the fraction of a second of their existence. Then, changing from capacitors which stored the electrical charge to a dynamo of special design, he more recently obtained fields of over 300,000 gauss and conducted experiments at that intensity.[10] The liquid hydrogen plant extended the range for his work down to the region of 14 degrees absolute (minus 259 degrees Celsius). But, although his laboratory was apparently successful, Kapitza felt that its status was unsettled and temporary. The DSIR support presumably might not go on forever and the extent of university interest in work only slightly connected with advanced teaching was problematical. Moreover, rising expenses were consuming his budget, his limited floor space could accommodate only two research students, and neither he nor his staff of four had any job security.

He therefore proposed to Rutherford, as chairman of the Magnetic Laboratory's advisory committee, the establishment of a permanent laboratory, housed in a structure of its own. This laboratory, he felt, should be a cross between a university laboratory like the Cavendish, where the staff spend a large portion of their time in teaching, and research institutions such as those in industry, where no teaching is done. The staff should devote most of their time to research but there should also be a steady flow of research students. Such a type of institution was the logical trend in science, Kapitza argued, pointing to the low temperature laboratories in Leyden and at the German Reichsanstalt, Pierre Weiss's magnetic laboratory in Strasbourg, and various high tension institutes. Only by developing such specialized centers would it be possible to afford such expensive scientific activities.

9. Kapitza letter to Rutherford, 16 Apr. 1930.
10. In 1964 the National Magnet Laboratory in Cambridge, Massachusetts, reported the attainment of the strongest *continuous* field ever achieved by man: 255,000 gauss (*Physics Today*, 17 [Dec. 1964], 79).

Again, Rutherford was in a position to help, for he saw the merit of establishing the Magnetic Laboratory as a permanent institution, with permanent staff and financing, and having a fixed place within the university. As President of the Royal Society, his known high opinion of Kapitza was of no small value, for the foremost scientific organization of Great Britain, in November 1930, appointed Kapitza "Messel Professor of the Royal Society" and became responsible for his salary. One month later the Royal Society offered to the University of Cambridge the sum of £15,000 for the building and equipment of a permanent magnetic and cryogenic laboratory, an offer soon accepted.

If Rutherford was aware of the criticism that Kapitza was doing more engineering than physics and that his work was interesting but had revealed nothing fundamental,[11] he paid it no heed. Kapitza was elected a Fellow of the Royal Society in 1929, the same year in which he was made a Corresponding Member of the Academy of Sciences of the USSR. When Stanley Baldwin, who succeeded Balfour as chancellor of Cambridge University, opened the Royal Society Mond Laboratory in early 1933, Kapitza was named its director. The closeness of the Mond to the Cavendish was represented by more than its physical proximity—it was nestled in the courtyard of the older laboratory, just through the great gate of the Cavendish. Unknown to Rutherford, Kapitza had the well-known sculptor, Eric Gill, carve a large crocodile in the bricks next to the Mond's entrance. In Russian folklore the crocodile is a symbol of power and terror, regarded with a mixture of awe and admiration. In Kapitza's eyes, Rutherford's quick temper, booming voice, and great leadership and research abilities clearly marked him as "the Crocodile," and his debt to his professor thus was symbolized in the carving.[12]

Unlike many other Russians who left their homeland after the Revolution, Kapitza was not an exile. He maintained his citizenship out of love for his country and sympathy with the Soviet government's goals of economic and social progress. Beginning in 1926, he paid visits to Russia almost every year, reestablishing a contact be-

11. Andrade, *Rutherford*, pp. 188–90.
12. Kapitza has never stated clearly his intent in commissioning this carving. But this explanation is given in Eve, *Rutherford*, pp. 369–70, and repeated by Danin, *Rutherford*, apparently with Kapitza's approval.

tween Russian and English science to which Rutherford had contributed years earlier through several students from that country. Kapitza's visits were usually made upon official invitation, for his government was aware of his growing reputation and sought his advice on scientific, technical, and educational matters. In 1926 the invitation came, along with a promise to permit his return to England, from Leon Trotsky, as President of the Collegium of the High Council of the People's Economy Board of Science and Technology.[13]

Similar invitations came in 1929 from Leo Kamenev, and in 1931 from Nikolai Bukharin, successors to Trotsky and like him doomed for crossing Stalin. Kamenev made Kapitza a consultant and placed him on an annual retainer, to obtain his advice on the establishment of a Physico-Technical Institute in Kharkov, the fifth largest city in the Soviet Union. This was a project that interested Kapitza, for he felt that scientific laboratories were concentrated too much in Moscow and Leningrad. For his part, Kamenev was explicit about regarding this association as a first step toward Kapitza's eventual permanent return to the Soviet Union. This question was, indeed, discussed on several occasions, Kapitza stressing that conditions in the USSR were not suitable for his work and that he could make more of a contribution to his country by working abroad, while the Soviet authorities apparently remained unconvinced.[14] While no record is preserved detailing this point of view, presumably they made a fuzzy distinction between pure and applied science and felt that Kapitza could materially help the economy. Moreover, and quite correctly, they probably recognized that a domestic laboratory would train primarily Russian citizens, which would raise the level of scientific competence in the country.

Bukharin was in England for the second International Congress of the History of Science and Technology when he visited Kapitza in Cambridge. Before he left Moscow, Agitation and Propaganda (Agitprop) chief Stetsky informed Bukharin that Stalin personally wished him to persuade Kapitza to return to the Soviet Union. Bu-

13. From biographical notes prepared about 1935 by Anna Kapitza.

14. Ibid.; also correspondence between Kapitza and Kamenev during 1929, quoted by Anna Kapitza in the same source.

kharin carried out this assignment, but Kapitza remained noncom-
mital. In none of these contacts with Trotsky, Kamenev, and
Bukharin was there any suggestion that Kapitza's permanent transferral would be other than voluntary, and he enjoyed the opportunities in his homeland to lecture and consult, and to visit his mother in
Leningrad.[15]

Without doubt, Kapitza also enjoyed his years in Cambridge. He
early established himself near the center of the laboratory social life,
and regular meetings of the Kapitza Club, a group of limited membership, were attended by many names now famous in the history of
science. Close friendships were made with, for example, John Cockcroft, who later helped him run the Mond Laboratory, and James
Chadwick, whose best man he was. (For Chadwick's wedding,
Kapitza borrowed a top hat from Rutherford's son-in-law, the mathematical physicist, Ralph Fowler.[16]) And, of course, Kapitza delighted in his closeness to Rutherford, to whom he could write,
when the latter was on a trip to New Zealand, "We are missing you
very much. I feel myself very uncomfortably as nobody is scolding
me sometimes a little."[17] On another occasion, Rutherford's sixtieth
birthday, Kapitza wrote:

> I hope you will kindly accept the small birthday present enclosed here-
> with. With the greatest respect to the high honours which you now
> hold and which makes us all feel proud for having such a "boss," but I
> have to admit that some times you challenge your high title. On numer-
> ous occasions I watched you extracting from your pocket a most dis-
> gracefully looking pencil or even more often a microscopic piece of
> such a pencil. I hope you will agree that since your head has to bear all
> the weight of a golden crown, it is unworthy to your hand to touch any
> more such wooden pencils.[18]

15. Arnosht (Ernest) Kolman, *We Should Not Have Lived That Way* (New York:
Chalidze Publications, 1982. In Russian), pp. 176–77.

16. Rutherford letter to Kapitza, 9 Oct. 1925, Rutherford Correspondence. Note
that "Correspondence" identifies sources from the letters half of the Rutherford collection in the Cambridge University Library. The otherwise unidentified items are
from the "Papers" half of this collection.

17. Kapitza letter to Rutherford, 11 Oct. 1925, Rutherford Correspondence.

18. Kapitza letter to Rutherford, 29 Aug. 1931, Rutherford Correspondence.

Kapitza, in fact, was quite conscious of Rutherford's many honors, perhaps even more so than Rutherford, and was particularly impressed by his professor's elevation to the peerage in 1931. "Can a foreigner," he reputedly asked a friend, "be made a member of the House of Lords?"

««« 2 »»»

Rutherford's "Power Politics"

Word of Kapitza's detention in Russia was brought back to Cambridge by Anna, his second wife and the daughter of Aleksei Krylov, whom he had married in 1927. They had traveled to their homeland in the summer of 1934, leaving her mother to care for their children in England. After attending the Mendeleev Conference and just a few days before his planned return, Kapitza was told by the Soviet authorities that he could not leave the country. His services, they explained, were now urgently needed by the Union.

When Rutherford heard the news, early in October, he wrote a calm but firm letter to the Soviet ambassador in London, suggesting that there had been some misunderstanding that could easily be rectified, but warning that otherwise scientific relations between their two countries would be damaged.[1] Ivan Maisky, the ambassador, wrote an equally calm but firm reply:

> In the Soviet Union the system in operation is that the Soviet Government plans not only the economy of the country, but also the distribution of labour, including the distribution of the scientific workers. While our scientific institutions were able to get along with the tasks assigned to them with the available scientists the Soviet Government did not raise any objections to Mr. Kapitza working in Cambridge. Now, however, as a result of the extraordinary development of the national economy of the U.S.S.R. due to the successful completion of the First and the energetic prosecution of the Second Five Year Plan, the available number of scientific workers does not suffice, and in these circumstances the Soviet Government has found it necessary to utilise for scientific activities within the country all of those scientists, Soviet

1. Rutherford letter to I. Maisky, 12 Oct. 1934.

citizens, who have hitherto been working abroad. Mr. Kapitza belongs to this category. He has now been offered highly responsible work in his particular field in the Soviet Union, which will enable him to develop fully his abilities as a scientist and a citizen of his country.[2]

Maisky, a talented individual, served in London for ten years and, following his retirement, published several volumes of memoirs, an unusual feat for a Soviet diplomat. He seems to have had no significant involvement in the Kapitza matter, the decisions being made and implemented in Moscow.

In hopes that the Russians could be amicably convinced to change their minds, Rutherford and the Cambridge University authorities kept news of Kapitza's plight within a relatively small group, preferring to exert their pressure privately. This tactic was motivated both by a reluctance to allow anti-Soviet newspapers to use the incident as a political weapon, and by an impression that, to save face, the Soviet officials would be intransigent once the case was made public.[3] Sir Robert Vansittart, Permanent Under-Secretary at the British Foreign Office, disagreed, however, feeling that the Russians would not hesitate to change their minds if they thought it to their advantage to do so. He offered to ask the ambassador in Moscow to approach the Soviet authorities, the representations being private, not official, since Kapitza was a Soviet citizen, but only if Rutherford, the University, the Royal Society, and the DSIR agreed to follow through with newspaper publicity, which he felt would help.[4] This offer, made in December 1934, apparently was not accepted, for publicity was held off for another four months.

Presumably, Rutherford was receiving advice in these matters, for his own experience in foreign affairs was obviously limited. Besides members of the laboratory and university, Anna Kapitza, a perceptive woman, no doubt was consulted about the best way to secure her husband's release, while Arnold D. McNair, Cambridge's prominent professor of international law and later an eminent international jurist, may have influenced Rutherford's behavior considera-

---

2. I. Maisky letter to Rutherford, 30 Oct. 1934.

3. Rutherford letter to J. F. Cameron, Vice-Chancellor of Cambridge University, 11 Dec. 1934.

4. J. F. Cameron letter to Rutherford, 12 Dec. 1934.

bly. But Rutherford also was developing his own expertise in the realm of foreign affairs, and not only because of this pupil's difficulties. Although science and politics were long felt to be incompatible, since May 1933 he had been president of the Academic Assistance Council, a group founded to aid the scholar-refugees, mostly Jews, fleeing Hitler's Germany.[5] The role involved both public statements and private solicitation of funds, and although the latter dominated it is likely that Rutherford increasingly trusted his own intuition. In any case, since he was always one to "listen to himself" primarily and since scientists had virtually never conducted their business in the newspapers, Vansittart's fallback condition so early in the game could be rejected. These Russian and German episodes, it might be added, impressed Rutherford (and many others) with the dangers that politics posed for science, and did nothing to enamor him of the former.

Kapitza for his part refused to engage in physics research under his present conditions of "captivity" and refrained from writing to his colleagues abroad, believing that such action would somehow weaken his case. Information about his unhappiness and desperate circumstances, therefore, reached English and other European scientists only through the letters to his wife, excerpts of which she gave to Rutherford, who circulated them among a limited group.

Rutherford, though sometimes characterized as a bluff, ready-for-action New Zealand farmer, in this matter exhibited the patience and deftness which had made him so successful in the laboratory. He wished to explore every possible avenue of private protest before having recourse to publicity, which he regarded as the last step. Before the university and the Royal Society made representations to the Soviet government, Rutherford felt that communications from individual scientists should be given a chance. In December 1934 he wrote to his former pupil and very close friend in Copenhagen, Niels Bohr, asking for his help.[6] Paul Langevin, a leading French leftist as well as an eminent physicist, having been told by Anna Kapitza of her husband's situation, had sent a letter to the proper authorities

5. Lord Beveridge, *A Defence of Free Learning* (London: Oxford University Press, 1959).

6. Rutherford letter to N. Bohr, 6 Dec. 1934.

P. M. S. Blackett, Peter Kapitza, Paul Langevin, Ernest Rutherford, and C. T. R. Wilson, in front of Cavendish Laboratory, on Free School Lane, June 1929. Courtesy of C. E. Wynn-Williams.

through the Soviet ambassador in Paris, and Bohr was now requested to do likewise. The man to contact, Rutherford believed, was Foreign Minister Maxim Litvinoff, who was abroad when the Kapitza decision was taken and who might therefore have a more flexible attitude. The theme to stress was that science could not be treated in such summary fashion without harm, and that by such action the USSR stood to lose more from the international community of scientists than she would gain.

Bohr had heard something about Kapitza's detention from George Gamow, another Soviet scientist working abroad, at that time in Bohr's Copenhagen laboratory but earlier in the Cavendish. He sidestepped the suggestion to write to Litvinoff, whom he did not know personally, and instead sent a letter to Bukharin, the prominent party theoretician and editor of the official newspaper *Pravda*, whom he had met on a journey to the USSR.[7] Rutherford appreci-

7. N. Bohr letter to Rutherford, 15 Dec. 1934.

ated this new avenue to the Soviet corridors of power,[8] just as he was grateful to Peter Debye, physics professor in Leipzig, for protesting to Joffé, one of the powers in the Soviet Academy of Sciences.[9] But Rutherford had yet in mind another means of tightening the screw. If leaders of the scientific world, say about a dozen men, sent a petition to the Soviet authorities, pointing out the dangers of the Kapitza episode prejudicing international scientific cooperation, this might be a very powerful document indeed. Since no one from Cambridge, as an interested party, should sign it and most certainly it should not be known that the idea of the petition came from Cambridge, would Bohr, a truly humane individual as well as a great scientist, undertake to organize it?[10] To spare his friend the trouble of composing the document, Rutherford enclosed a draft in English[11] and, to obscure its British origin, a translation into French which was meant for circulation.

Rutherford took these pains to make the petition appear spontaneous because he recognized that the Russians would consider any of his efforts as part of his duty. He again suggested Litvinoff as the target, the foreign minister being most sensitive to the danger of international repercussions. In view of the recent Franco-Russian entente, he felt that some prominent French politician might serve as an effective intermediary, hence the draft in French, and asked Bohr to seek Langevin's aid in choosing the proper politician. Bohr duly wrote to the French physicist in early January 1935 to ask whether Langevin would contact Litvinoff personally, as well as to get advice about the petition, for he was afraid that the semipublic nature of the latter course might crystallize the matter in an unfavorable position.[12]

Another factor which cast doubt on the efficacy of such a petition was the circumstance that it would be weakened by the inclusion *or*

8. Rutherford letter to N. Bohr, 19 Dec. 1934.
9. P. Debye letter to Rutherford, 29 Dec. 1934, and Rutherford letter to P. Debye, 11 Jan. 1935. Another spontaneous protest was Ira S. Bowen and Roscoe G. Dickinson letter to the American Russian Institute of Southern California, Los Angeles, 17 May 1935, Bowen collection, Archives, California Institute of Technology.
10. Rutherford letter to N. Bohr, 19 Dec. 1934.
11. See Appendix.
12. N. Bohr letter to Rutherford, 7 Jan. 1935.

the absence of signatures from German scientists. Hitler's Nazi government was actively ejecting Jewish scholars from their positions, an action that differed greatly from the Russian approach. Although only 1 percent of the population, Jews in Germany held one-eighth of the professorships and had won one-quarter of the Nobel Prizes in that country. Their influence was felt to be too great, and their interests were associated with distasteful pacifism, internationalism, communism, the hated Versailles Treaty, and Germany's desperate economic condition. Virulent anti-Semitism therefore found other social attitudes sympathetic to its goal of "cleansing" Aryan society. Because almost all university teachers and institute personnel were civil servants, the government could and did dismiss or force the resignations of virtually all Jews in such employ. More than 1,500 scholars lost their positions; this included about 14 percent of those in German higher education, and at least 25 percent of those in physics during 1932–33.[13] Given this situation in the Third Reich, Bohr recognized that the anti-Nazi Germans could hardly criticize the Soviet government when they felt their own was behaving so deplorably, whereas the pro-Nazi Germans who might sign the petition would be accused of double standards. It was truly an ironic situation, for both governments were treating scientists badly, but by comparison the Russians merited more praise (or less condemnation), for at least they wished to keep their citizens.

Bohr's resultant uncertainty about the wisdom of the petition approach, coupled with Langevin's characteristic disinclination to respond to his mail, or even to a telegram that Bohr subsequently sent, doomed this means of pressure to a stillbirth.[14] By the end of April 1935, Rutherford was obliged to consider this avenue closed.[15]

Earlier in the year Rutherford had seriously considered sending William Webster, a postdoctoral research worker in the Mond Labo-

13. Alan D. Beyerchen, *Scientists Under Hitler* (New Haven: Yale University Press, 1977), pp. 14, 44; Norman Bentwich, *The Rescue and Achievement of Refugee Scholars* (The Hague: Nijhoff, 1953), p. 2; Charles Weiner, "A new site for the seminar," in Donald Fleming and Bernard Bailyn, eds., *The Intellectual Migration: Europe and America 1930–1960* (Cambridge, Mass.: Harvard University Press, 1969).
14. N. Bohr letter to Rutherford, 27 Apr. 1935.
15. Rutherford letter to N. Bohr, 30 Apr. 1935.

ratory, to Russia to interview Kapitza.[16] They were greatly concerned about Kapitza's mental health and were not certain whether he was able to write freely or feared secret police censorship. It was known that two detectives kept him under surveillance and a third person was present at all important discussions.[17] The problem for Webster was to justify a midwinter trip to Moscow in the questionnaire required before a visa would be issued. If he did not mention Kapitza and then asked to see him once he was in Russia, he would likely be accused of deceit and his request denied. Alternatively, if he specified a visit to Kapitza in the questionnaire, the reaction might range from denial of the visa to approval, but if the latter, Kapitza might be moved about so as to prevent their meeting. In the end, this plan of attack was abandoned, largely because it was judged dangerous to Kapitza.

Compromise plans, designed to salvage part of Kapitza's career in England, yet save Russia's face, were offered to both the Soviets and Rutherford by such men as Peter Debye[18] and Harold Laski,[19] professor of political science at the London School of Economics and well-known spokesman for socialism. Such plans provided six months each year in each country, or two final years in England before Kapitza's honor-bound permanent return to his homeland, or at least a month in Britain to wind up his affairs. But if any were seriously pursued by either side, no record remains.

The final type of approach considered before newspapers publicized the matter was official representation by the British institutions concerned, through their government. As mentioned earlier, Rutherford preferred individual and personal efforts first, largely because he believed that the Soviet government would regard the university and the Royal Society as British government annexes, but also because he was aware that the two countries were not on the best of diplomatic terms.[20] Still, plans were laid for a delegation consisting of Vice-Chancellor J. F. Cameron and Rutherford representing the university, and Secretary Frank Smith and President

16. W. L. Webster letter to Rutherford, 6 Feb. 1935.
17. Rutherford letter to P. A. M. Dirac, 28 Jan. 1935.
18. P. Debye letter to Rutherford, 29 Dec. 1934.
19. W. L. Webster letter to Rutherford, 6 Feb. 1935.
20. Rutherford letter to N. Bohr, 19 Dec. 1934.

F. Gowland Hopkins (Rutherford's successor) representing the Royal Society, to call on Stanley Baldwin, who then was Lord President of the Council (he became prime minister for the third time in June 1935), and who, since 1930, had been the university's chancellor (essentially a titular position).[21] Whether these plans were ever put into action is not clear, for as late as March 1935, Rutherford and the others decided not to approach Anthony Eden before the Lord Privy Seal's visit to Russia, because they felt he would not want to be bothered with such a relatively minor matter during his important talks with the Soviets.[22]

These talks, which went far toward reestablishing cordial relations between the two countries, were much desired by the British, who watched with alarm Hitler's actions on the Continent. The Soviets, no less, welcomed these discussions, for they too were looking about for allies. Between World Wars I and II the United Kingdom was concerned mostly with domestic affairs. Disappointment over the League of Nations' failure, coupled with such pressing problems as economic recovery from World War I, the rise of socialism, Ireland, and India, caused the nation to turn inward. The Soviets, as will be mentioned in the next chapter, were likewise obsessed with domestic matters.

But there were contacts between the two countries over the years since the Revolution, and one of these possibly had bearing on Kapitza's situation because of its technical orientation. Anglo-Russian diplomatic and trade relations were repeatedly severed and restored and threatened during the 1920s and early 1930s by a series of incidents, including the 1924 Zinoviev letter, a seditious document allegedly signed by the Russian president of the Third International which contributed to the downfall of the incumbent British Labour government,[23] charges of espionage against the Soviet trade mission in London, and Soviet indignation over accusations of slavery conditions in their Siberian timber trade.

Then, in March 1933, six British engineers of the Metropolitan

21. F. E. Smith letter to Rutherford, 14 Dec. 1934, and F. G. Hopkins letter to Rutherford, 14 Dec. 1934.
22. Rutherford letter to A. D. McNair, 11 Mar. 1935.
23. Lewis Chester, Stephen Fay, and Hugo Young, *The Zinoviev Letter* (New York: Lippincott, 1968).

Vickers Company were arrested while working in the USSR and brought to trial on charges of sabotage and espionage. They were accused of bribing Soviet citizens to engage (successfully) in "wrecking activities" at electrical power plants, for example, by introducing foreign materials into motors and turbines, allowing off-line boilers to freeze, overlooking structural defects found in machinery supplied by the English company, and so forth, the goal being to lower electricity production. They were accused further of gathering information about production from military factories powered by electricity from the plants to which they had access, and plotting with the twelve Soviet defendants means to limit electricity still more in case of war.[24] At their trial before a special session of the Supreme Court of the USSR, with Andrei Vyshinsky prosecuting, one engineer was acquitted, three were convicted and deported, and the others given prison sentences of two and three years. They served only two months, however, and were then deported.[25]

British public opinion was much aroused by what was considered a staged manifestation of Soviet displeasure. The presumed reason for their anger was the unilateral renunciation by England of the 1930 trade agreement with the USSR, made necessary by the former's abandonment of free trade in favor of protection at the Imperial Conference in Ottawa in the autumn of 1932. When the engineers were first arrested, the British ambassador, Sir Esmond Ovey, made such strong protests to Foreign Minister Litvinoff that he considered his subsequent usefulness in Moscow at an end and asked for his own recall. Ovey's successor, Aretas Akers-Douglas, Viscount Chilston, was able to establish amicable personal relations with Litvinoff, which favorably colored their countries' diplomatic exchanges; the Eden mission to Moscow a year later was meant to consolidate these advances. Yet, with this background of mutual Anglo-Russian suspicion, it is not hard to understand the low value Rutherford placed upon representations by his government on Kapitza's behalf.

Thus, despite some unfulfilled plans, for diplomatic intervention and the petition, and some actions completed, such as personal com-

---

24. *Wrecking Activities at Power Stations in the Soviet Union* (Translation of the official verbatim trial record; Moscow: State Law Publishing House, 1933).
25. *The Times*, 20, 21, 24, 31 Mar. and 5, 6 July 1933.

munications to the Soviet authorities, little was accomplished in the early months of 1935. One Cambridge colleague suggested a boy-cott of the International Physiological Congress, scheduled for that summer in Moscow. He reasoned that the Russians, justly proud of Pavlov, the greatest of their living scientists, might be brought around if his meeting was endangered.[26] But Rutherford, sensing that Kapitza would not be freed and wishing to make his position in Russia as tolerable as possible, apparently vetoed this idea.[27] Still, Rutherford would not admit defeat in his efforts, and when S. B. Cahan, Counsellor of the Russian Embassy (and believed to be the GPU agent assigned to watch over the embassy staff), visited Cam-bridge in March with an offer to purchase Kapitza's apparatus, Rutherford was disinclined to accept.[28] He did, however, concede that if there was no hope of Kapitza's release, he would make every effort to help him resume his work in the Soviet Union.[29] But this was a bargaining point for concessions.

The matter finally became public when the *News Chronicle* head-lined the story on 24 April 1935. How the paper learned of the case is unknown, for despite mounting fears that Kapitza was near a men-tal breakdown[30] and that publicity was their last resort, Anna Kap-itza and Cockcroft considered requesting the paper not to pub-lish.[31] They were dissuaded from this plan by Frank Smith, who as Secretary of the DSIR, as well as of the Royal Society, was felt to be more familiar with life outside academia.[32] It would be futile, Smith counseled. The *News Chronicle* may, in fact, have picked up its story from the anti-Soviet *Last News*, published by émigrés in Paris, the previous 9 March. This obscure paper seems to have carried the only public statement of Kapitza's detention before the wide coverage in England.

Other newspapers soon made Kapitza a household name, and the details of his career and present troubles spilled over their pages. A

26. A. D. McNair letter to Rutherford, 11 Mar. 1935.
27. Rutherford letter to A. D. McNair, 18 Mar. 1935.
28. Ibid.; also sheet of biographical details on Cahan.
29. Rutherford letter to P. Leigh-Smith, 26 Apr. 1935.
30. J. D. Cockcroft letter to Rutherford, 14 Apr. 1935.
31. F. E. Smith letter to Rutherford, 24 Apr. 1935.
32. Ibid.

measure of his scientific eminence was seen in the fact that he occupied one of the very few Royal Society professorships, the others held by A. V. Hill, O. W. Richardson, E. D. Adrian, and G. I. Taylor, outstanding individuals all. Another point featured was Kapitza's innovativeness, typified by his development of a special dynamo to produce extreme magnetic fields, and his novel method for making large quantities of liquid helium more easily than before.[33] One of the grand old men of British science, Sir Oliver Lodge, expressed his disappointment with the Russian action, for both he and Einstein hoped that Kapitza would use his newly erected apparatus in Cambridge to test for the existence of the luminiferous ether.[34] With the intense fields he could produce, they felt that Kapitza might be able to create a "whirlpool" in the ether, and then measure the velocity of light with and against the direction of this flow, an experiment reminiscent of one performed by Lodge at the end of the nineteenth century using heavy flywheels to carry the ether about. In fact, Kapitza had been reluctant to undertake this test for a medium in which few any longer believed because the expected effect would be of the same order as the experimental error. The data would not be decisive and would only add more fuel to a moribund controversy.[35]

The newspapers naturally contacted the Soviet Embassy in London, which issued the following statement:

> Peter Kapitza is a citizen of the U.S.S.R., educated and trained as a scientist at the expense of his country. He was sent to England to continue his studies and research work. Actually he stayed in England rather longer than he should have done.
>
> Now the time has arrived when the Soviet urgently needs all her scientists. So when Professor Kapitza came home last summer he was appointed as director of an important new research station which is being built at Moscow.

---

33. *Manchester Guardian*, 25 Apr. 1935. For information about the helium liquefier, see J. G. Crowther, "Near absolute zero," *Scientific American*, 151 (Dec. 1934), 300–02.

34. *News Chronicle*, 25 Apr. 1935.

35. D. ter Haar, ed., *Collected Papers of P. L. Kapitza* (Oxford: Pergamon, 1967). vol. 3, p. 194.

Professor Kapitza is being treated with all the dignity due to a distinguished scientist. He has been given a very nice house and a motorcar.

There has been no application of any kind from the British Government for the professor's return to Great Britain, although we gather that Cambridge would very naturally like to have him back.

Cambridge would no doubt like to have all the world's greatest scientists in its laboratories in much the same way as the Soviet would like to have Lord Rutherford and other of your great physicists in her laboratories.

The plain fact is that Professor Kapitza is a Soviet citizen and his country needs him.[36]

Rutherford was also interviewed, and called attention to the brutal fashion in which the Soviets acted. Their government might be able successfully to order a man to become an expert bricklayer, he said, but it is not sensible to suppose that they can cage a man in Moscow, away from his home, family, and work, and order him to become a great physicist. Kapitza, "if not a genius," Rutherford added, "had the brain of a physicist and the ability of a mechanician, a combination so rarely wedded in one brain that it made him something of a phenomenon."[37]

Anna Kapitza, also interviewed by the journalists, naturally was more concerned with the state of Peter's highly strung personality. "The whole affair," she noted, "has caused great mental pain and anxiety to both my husband and myself. When the Soviet Government requested my husband to remain in Russia he was at once confronted with a difficult decision," namely, his loyalty to his country versus his loyalty to those in England who had shown confidence in him, and his reluctance to interrupt his work when he was about to commence an important series of experiments. "To a man of my husband's temperament the sudden change of his plans has been a grave shock which has severely upset him. In his present state of mind he is not in a position to do any serious scientific work."[38]

The legality of the Russian action and a grudging sympathy with certain of their goals moderated what little editorial criticism

36. *News Chronicle*, 24 Apr. 1935.
37. *Observer*, 28 Apr. 1935.
38. *News Chronicle*, 25 Apr. 1935.

appeared. The *Cambridge Review*, for example, contained this observation:

> It is at least more intelligible that a country should insist on keeping its scientists because they are its citizens, than that it should expel them for racial reasons. . . . But the Russian Government have unfortunately applied to this case an intense nationalism which is not in their own best interests,—let alone the blow which it inflicts upon science that knows neither creed nor race.[39]

British Marxist scientists, such as J. D. Bernal, J. B. S. Haldane, Hyman Levy, and Julian Huxley, who were active in the Social Relations of Science movement, apparently made no public statements. Their admiration for some of Russia's goals presumably conflicted with this affront to their scientific ideals.[40]

To keep the pressure on, and to present his case to that most influential segment of British opinion which read *The Times*, Rutherford wrote a letter to that august newspaper, which was printed on 29 April 1935.[41] Yet this summary of Kapitza's career and of his present difficulties was directed as much to the Soviet Embassy as to Britons. For Rutherford's tone was sympathetic and conciliatory; he hoped still to open the eyes of the Moscow authorities and have them reverse their decision. "May we hope that the Soviet Government," he asked, "which has given so many proofs of its interest in the development of science, will pursue a generous and long-sighted policy, and will see its way to meet the wishes of scientific men, not only of this country, but throughout the world, by enabling Kapitza to choose the environment in which he can most effectively utilize the special creative gifts with which he is endowed?"

This appeal to the Soviet conscience was criticized by B. Perott, a Russian émigré physician living in London, who was a friend of Kapitza. As Bolsheviks have no moral faculties, he maintained, the effort would be useless. Perott suggested, however, two persons whose influence might be significant: the Bolshevik writer, Maxim Gorky, residing on Capri, and, quite oppositely, the only "person in

---

39. *Cambridge Review*, 3 May 1935.
40. For a brief description of this movement see Robert Filner, "The roots of political activism in British science," *Bulletin of the Atomic Scientists*, 32 (Jan. 1976), 25–29.
41. See Appendix.

Soviet-Russia who fearlessly and openly denied the Bolshevik creed and has never been touched by them," the physiologist, Pavlov.[42] Rutherford knew Gorky personally but there is no record of any appeal to him. Kapitza, in Moscow, had been in contact with Pavlov, in whose laboratory he at first planned to begin a new career in physiology, but it is not known whether Pavlov was capable of extending more than sympathy to him.[43]

Another writer whose name entered the story in the spring of 1935 was H. G. Wells, who was fascinated by the newspaper accounts and wished to hear the details firsthand from Anna Kapitza. As president of the Pen Club, he was soon to go to Barcelona for a meeting and proposed to discuss the matter in his address. Kapitza's plight must be kept in the news so as to bring continued pressure on the Soviets, Wells told Anna, who judged him more interested in the idea of freedom of the individual than in her husband. When Anna suggested that it would be a rather unpleasant conclusion if Peter were placed in a prison camp, Wells agreed and said it was quite possible. But, he added, the Soviets are completely incomprehensible and one cannot predict their reactions.[44]

At this same time, Rutherford was finally in touch with his government, specifically P. Leigh-Smith of the Foreign Office and Stanley Baldwin. The previous December, Henry Dale, one of the Secretaries of the Royal Society, had been told by the Foreign Office that they would be willing to make unofficial representations in Moscow, if formally requested.[45] As we have seen, this course of action was temporarily rejected. Now, with better relations following the Eden visit and with no cards left up his sleeve, Rutherford authorized Leigh-Smith to speak unofficially and personally to the Soviet Embassy Counsellor in London, Cahan. For reasons unknown, Rutherford now believed that the Russians recognized that they had acted unwisely and that Kapitza would not be of as much use to them as originally thought.[46] Consequently, he wished to keep as

42. B. Perott letter to Rutherford, 29 Apr. 1935.
43. Rutherford letter to B. Perott, 2 May 1935.
44. Anna Kapitza letter to Rutherford, 16 May 1935.
45. P. Leigh-Smith letter to Rutherford, 25 Apr. 1935.
46. Rutherford letter to P. Leigh-Smith, 26 Apr. 1935; Rutherford letter to F. E. Smith, 26 Apr. 1935; Rutherford letter to S. Baldwin, 29 Apr. 1935.

many lines of communication open as possible, hoping that his olive branch would permit the Soviets to retire gracefully from their positions. During May 1935 Baldwin discussed the affair with Eden but no action followed,[47] although through Leigh-Smith the embassy in Moscow made inquiries, only to receive the standard formal—and negative—reply.[48] In the end, the diplomatic efforts came to as little as the other techniques.

Public opinion could not be much inflamed by the issue, for Kapitza was, after all, legally detained by his own country, and in conditions that not all would consider bad. Moreover, after many years of a bad press the Soviets had gained widespread cheers shortly before for the rescue of a hundred men, women, and children adrift for a few months on an Arctic ice floe after their ship had gone down. The world thrilled to the massive effort by the Soviet government, all the more because it was unexpected from a country which seemed to regard human life as cheap, and Ambassador Maisky regarded the "*Chelyuskin* epic" as a major breakthrough in changing Britons' attitudes toward his country. Kapitza's plight was not significant enough to change this attitude. For Maisky, in fact, Kapitza seems to have posed no problem. His diplomatic contacts in London steadily improved, and even such a former foe as Beaverbrook, the "press lord," invited him to lunch in June 1935. Hitler was now the Soviet enemy; all else was secondary. Kapitza's detention is not even mentioned in Maisky's autobiography.[49]

Nor did the ranks of British science maintain a unified stiff upper lip. There was, indeed, one flexible lower jaw that must have given Rutherford wry amusement. For Henry Armstrong, who thirty years earlier was virtually the only supporter Lord Kelvin had in opposing Rutherford and Soddy's explanation of radioactivity as an atomic transmutation, but whose opposition was based on a refusal to accept conclusions drawn from experiments on unweighable (and even invisible!) quantities of matter,[50] now stood in opposition to

47. S. Baldwin letter to Rutherford, 5 May 1935.

48. Rutherford letter to P. Leigh-Smith, 23 May 1935. Also see Foreign Office notes and correspondence, Public Record Office, London, FO 371/19470, folios 41–66.

49. I. Maisky, *Who Helped Hitler?* (London: Hutchinson, 1964).

50. L. Badash, "How the newer alchemy was received," *Scientific American*, 215 (Aug. 1966), 88–95.

those who regarded Kapitza's situation as a bad thing. Armstrong, a chemist of the old school, with a wide reputation for being willing to engage in controversy on almost any topic, spoke as the senior Fellow of the Royal Society, a distinction reached by his longevity. In a letter to *The Times* on 7 May[51] he professed a failure to see any signs of "severe shock to the scientific world," described by Rutherford in his own letter. Instead, Armstrong found a feeling of relief, particularly among younger British scientists whose opportunities for advancement were blocked by imported "foreign labour."[52]

By this phrase Armstrong no doubt evoked visions not only of foreign individuals invited to fill certain professorships—a reasonably common occurrence—but also of the recent flood of refugee scientists from Germany. Many were already well known in their profession, and their potential candidacy for vacant positions, if based solely on merit, inevitably would preclude the election of some native Britons. In an academic and industrial world already suffering from the Depression, the specter of increased likelihood of unemployment stirred feelings that conflicted with the intuitive desire to assist Hitler's unfortunate victims.

It is likely that Armstrong was also the only one with courage enough to verbalize another unexpressed sentiment. Just as he had been educated abroad and then had played a role in making English chemistry independent of German help, Armstrong felt that Kapitza owed it to his country to aid in its development, especially if the Russians were as technically inept as commonly claimed and Kapitza was a mechanical wizard. He would not be especially missed either in the nation that produced Faraday and others of great mechanical skill. Surely, Armstrong continued, Kapitza's genius had been overrated, and far too much importance had been "attached to the doings of the atom-smashing brigade led by Lord Rutherford." Previewing the attitude to be encountered in the 1950s and 1960s, he suggested sending the atomic scientists into the Sahara for about ten years, while research on significant problems in applied science was supported. There were more important things to be done than "magnetizing atoms to destruction."

51. See Appendix.
52. Evidence in support of Armstrong's claim is lacking, but in view of Rutherford's leading position in British science it might have been impolitic for a younger scientist to voice such opinions publicly.

Armstrong also took issue with the letter F. Gowland Hopkins had written to *The Times*, in which the Soviets were chastised for being indifferent to the Royal Society's awkward position in having spent trust funds for purposes suddenly terminated.[53] His old friends Mond and Messel would not, he growled, have approved of the way in which the Royal Society had spent their benefactions on a laboratory and for academic-type professorships. And, further, if Kapitza was a Soviet citizen, why had he been made a Fellow of the Royal Society?[54]

While Armstrong did, in fact, raise several points worthy of discussion, he had been a gadfly for so long that no one seems to have paid any attention to him. Rutherford, certainly, was too occupied looking for signs from Moscow to bother with this brushfire in his backyard. But as the month of May wore on, it grew increasingly apparent to him that the efforts on a variety of fronts had been to no avail, and that the Soviet government had no intention of releasing Kapitza from his captivity.[55] Soon, he would have to admit that the die was cast.

53. *The Times*, 1 May 1935. See Appendix.

54. The *Yearbook of the Royal Society* for 1929, the year in which Kapitza was elected a Fellow, contains no eligibility requirements. For the special honorary category of Foreign Membership, however, it is specified that they be "neither natives nor inhabitants of His Majesty's dominions." The implication, therefore, is that Kapitza, who was an inhabitant of England, was legally eligible for Fellowship. It is of interest that the requirements are now detailed and that Kapitza would not be eligible; the candidates must be subjects of Her Majesty or citizens of the Irish Republic. This change was made after World War II, when the large number of eminent refugee-scientists in Britain threatened to cause exclusion of worthy British candidates.

55. By contrast, science had become so important to the Soviet government by 1973 that the international protests against anticipated actions against Andrei Sakharov, for his human rights activities, are given much credit for protecting him.

««« 3 »»»

Science and the Soviets

Thus far in this narrative one question has been omitted: Why did the Soviet Union feel compelled in 1934 to reclaim forcibly one of her citizens? The letter from Ambassador Maisky and the embassy press release said quite simply that the country needed her scientists. While no doubt true, this was not the only explanation in public and private circulation.

Perhaps the most fanciful was the rumor that Kapitza had engineered the entire episode himself, with ulterior motives.[1] What these motives were alleged to be is not clear, but possibly Kapitza's detractors assumed that he desired to head the larger and potentially more prestigious laboratory promised him in Moscow and, because of the debt he owed to British science, could not appear to leave the newly constructed Mond Laboratory voluntarily. No one seems to have believed this disreputable story enough to have put it into print, but around Christmas 1934 it gained a certain degree of hushed-voice currency.

One nuance in the direction of credibility was the suggestion that Kapitza had long ago agreed with his countrymen to return if he were given a large laboratory and excellent working conditions, and that the Soviets had merely made up his mind for him as to the question of timing.[2] This was a version put forward by young university people of "advanced" ideas, although Rutherford believed it to be disseminated through the official channels of the USSR in Britain.

1. F. G. Hopkins letter to Rutherford, 14 Dec. 1934.
2. J. Webb, private secretary to the editor of *The Times*, letter to Rutherford, 25 Apr. 1935.

The matter, he felt, was causing English communists considerable embarrassment and they were seeking to gloss over it.[3]

Yet more credible was the belief that the Soviets suspected Kapitza of performing war work for the British government, in which case they would certainly prefer that he work at home. Kapitza himself so interpreted the motivation of his government,[4] and Rutherford was forced to agree.[5] Nor was the charge so improbable to Russians suspicious by nature, for Kapitza, in furnishing his laboratory with specially constructed electrical apparatus, had had extensive dealings with that company of evil repute in the Soviet Union—Metropolitan Vickers[6]—and he had received considerable support from that agency of the Crown—the Department of Scientific and Industrial Research. Not only would the Soviets *prefer* to receive the benefits of any war work he happened to do, they possibly decided that he could be distinctly useful.

There was even documentary evidence upon which to base a realistic belief that Kapitza was engaged in military research, although it was rather dated and its existence was not likely to be widely known. More than ten years earlier he had taken out a provisional patent entitled "Improvements in Electric Storage Apparatus."[7] The name of Sir Henry F. Heath, Secretary of the Imperial Trust for the Encouragement of Scientific and Industrial Research, appeared on the patent too, presumably because the research had been supported by DSIR funds. The work, of course, concerned Kapitza's efforts to create intense magnetic fields for his research purposes by the instantaneous discharge of electricity. But, in the customary practice of laying claim to all other possible applications when preparing a patent claim, he had noted that the intense field so produced could be used to discharge a projectile from a gun, with a velocity satisfactory for current needs and with greater precision than was obtainable with

3. Rutherford letter to the editor of *The Times*, 26 Apr. 1935.
4. Kapitza's statement of 19 Aug. 1935, recorded by E. D. Adrian.
5. Rutherford letter to P. A. M. Dirac, 28 Jan. 1935. Glenn Millikan letter to his parents, Mr. and Mrs. Robert A. Millikan, 6 Mar. 1935, G. Millikan collection, Archives, California Institute of Technology.
6. A. D. McNair letter to Rutherford, 11 Mar. 1935.
7. British Provisional Patent Specification, no. 22390/23, dated 5 Sept. 1923. Also see DSIR Advisory Council, papers submitted at meeting of 30 Nov. 1927, Public Record Office, London, class DSIR 2.31.

explosives. Yet, in 1935, this fascinating idea was not mentioned by anyone, and even Kapitza seems to have forgotten he ever suggested it.

An English magazine called *The Aeroplane* saw the "plot" in its own area of expertise. Kapitza was detained in Russia, it said, because of his great skill in liquid helium production, skill useful to a belligerent nation. "Given adequate supplies of helium, airships can be built which will be impregnable to anything except large bombs, and will be so capable of defending themselves that ordinary interceptor fighters will be useless against them."[8]

Not all the speculation centered on military application of Kapitza's knowledge. Another category may be called industrial. Kapitza's work on the low temperature liquefaction of gases had led him to an interest in the production of oxygen in industrial quantities. The cheapest means, he felt, would be to liquefy air and then distill it.

As one who used powerful electrical currents in his experimental work, Kapitza was also recognized as an expert upon this subject. And as who was loath to leave all praise in the unskilled hands of others, he no doubt made his comrades in Russia well aware of these abilities during his visits. Rutherford clearly felt that the "sudden action of the Soviets in commandeering Kapitza was due to their belief that his work had very important and immediate applications for industrial purposes."[9] More specifically, Rutherford had learned that Kapitza, "in one of his expansive moods in Russia, told the Soviet engineers that he himself would be able to alter the whole face of electrical engineering in his lifetime."[10] One of the reasons for Rutherford's hope of Kapitza's release during the spring of 1935 was his understanding that the Russians soon recognized the emptiness of his protégé's claim. But he must have underestimated the serious attention such a boast would receive in the Soviet Union, a country whose leader and prophet, Lenin, had said repeatedly that the success of socialism will come through electrical power.[11]

8. *The Aeroplane*, 48 (1 May 1935), 487–88.
9. Rutherford letter to P. Leigh-Smith, 26 Apr. 1935.
10. Rutherford letter to F. E. Smith, 26 Apr. 1935.
11. Such remarks were quoted widely, e.g., in *Wrecking Activities at Power Stations in the Soviet Union* (Moscow: State Law Publishing House, 1933), pt. 3, p. 39, and in Benjamin I. Weitz et al., eds., *Electric Power Development in the U.S.S.R.* (in English;

Further evidence that life is not simple and motives may be complex lies in the circumstance that there were other Russian scientists working abroad whom their government wished to return home. Some consented, voluntarily or under pressure, and some refused. Among the latter were Vladimir Ipatieff and George Gamow. Ipatieff, who had been a lieutenant-general in the Imperial Army as well as a chemistry teacher, was over sixty years of age by 1930. His significant research work in catalysis, particularly problems associated with petroleum refining, led to his assignment in charge of the mobilization of the Russian chemical industry at the outbreak of World War I. Such was his success that the new Soviet government also made use of his services in very high positions. But it was an uneasy decade following the war, and despite his administrative and research contributions he was warned by a friend in 1930 that he was on the list of those to be arrested. Since five military technical engineers, former students and colleagues of his, had been shot without a trial in 1929, and other friends and co-workers had also been arrested, such a warning could not be ignored. When, in June 1930, Ipatieff had the good fortune to be sent abroad for a scientific meeting, and his wife was permitted to accompany him, he thereupon resolved not to return.[12] After settling that same year in the United States, he was approached several times by the Soviet ambassador in Washington and by government trade representatives urging him to reconsider, but he chose to remain in America until his death in 1952.[13]

George Gamow was one of a number of distinguished young scientists from many countries who were enabled to travel and study abroad during the 1920s and 1930s by Rockefeller Foundation fellowships. Leaving his native Russia in the spring of 1928, he spent a

Moscow: Inra Publishing Society, 1936), p. 4. Weitz cites as his source V. I. Lenin, *Collected Works*, vol. 26, p. 434. Loren Graham, *The Soviet Academy of Sciences and the Communist Party, 1927–1932* (Princeton: Princeton University Press, 1967), p. 70, quotes Lenin's slogan as "Communism is Soviet power plus electrification of the whole country."

12. Herman Pines, "Ipatieff: man and scientist," *Science*, 157 (14 July 1967), 166–70. Also see V. N. Ipatieff, *The Life of a Chemist* (Stanford: Stanford University Press, 1946).

13. H. Pines letter to the author, 8 Aug. 1967.

year in Göttingen and in Bohr's Copenhagen laboratory. After only a few months back in Leningrad, he was once more the wandering scholar, this time spending a total of a year and a half in Cambridge and again in Copenhagen. It was during one of these visits to Rutherford's laboratory that his quantum mechanical arguments showed Cockcroft and Walton that nuclei could be disrupted in their planned accelerator at much lower voltages than originally believed.

Upon his return to Leningrad in the spring of 1931, Gamow encountered a changed situation. Stalin's new policy declared that "proletarian science" and "capitalistic science" were mutually hostile, much as "Aryan science" shortly challenged "Jewish science" in Germany, and Gamow was subsequently refused his passport to attend meetings and give lectures in Rome, Copenhagen, Ann Arbor, Michigan, and other centers of physics activity. But in the fall of 1933 he was surprised to receive a document from the Kremlin advising him that he could attend the traditional and prestigious Solvay Congress, held in Brussels. And, like Ipatieff, he was allowed, contrary to usual Soviet practice, to take his wife with him. This was, however, not some bureaucratic oversight; he had appealed successfully to the only high-standing communist he knew, the same Nikolai Bukharin mentioned earlier, who was purged and executed by Stalin in 1938.

Once in Brussels, Gamow told Bohr that he had no intention of returning to Russia. Had they continued to let him go and come freely, he said, he would have been happy to remain a citizen of his homeland. But once they obstructed his movements, he could not go back. To his amazement, Bohr protested that he must. And then the story came out. Recognizing that Gamow would not be permitted to leave the USSR under ordinary circumstances, Bohr had asked Paul Langevin to intercede with Moscow. Langevin, besides being an eminent French physicist and leftist, as mentioned before, was permanent president of the Solvay Physics Congresses and also chairman of the scientific liaison committee between France and the Soviet Union. As such, he carried significant weight in the Kremlin, but, as Bohr realized, Langevin's credibility depended upon Gamow's return. Gamow's dilemma, a choice between violating someone's trust in him and a future in an oppressive environment, was resolved by Marie Curie. Childhood hatred of Imperial Russian rule of her native Poland had inclined her to the political left and, because of her scientific and ideological sympathies with Langevin, she was able to persuade her good friend to give Gamow his "moral freedom."[14] Langevin, it seems likely, was not especially pleased with his own role in the matter and most probably deliberately ignored Bohr's appeal on Kapitza's behalf a year later.

Permitted to stay in the West, Gamow spent a few months in Paris and in Cambridge and then sailed for the United States, where he lived until his death in 1968. Interestingly, he revealed his intentions to Kapitza, by then a close friend, not long before the latter departed for Russia in the summer of 1934. Whether Kapitza attempted to dissuade his younger colleague is not known, but Gamow recalled that he urged Kapitza to secure a written promise that he would be permitted to return to England. Kapitza, however, claimed that this formality was no longer required and, in fact, implied that the Soviet government had let him know it felt insulted by this annual request. Thus, Kapitza left on his visit without the customary agreement, with the results described in this volume.[15]

The significant connection between the activities of these two men is that a number of people, Kapitza included, believed that Gamow's defection was materially responsible for Kapitza's detention. This was, for example, the theme of the article that appeared in the *Last News*, the anti-Soviet newspaper published by Russians in Paris, which first broke the Kapitza story. Gamow, the paper said, was permitted abroad only because Professors Joffé and Kapitza stood as warrantors for his return. When Kapitza himself went to Russia, unaware of Gamow's decision, he was kept there as a hostage for Gamow's return.[16] It must be pointed out that this version differs greatly from Gamow's own narrative of the events as described above, as to both Kapitza's prior knowledge of Gamow's defection and the circumstances under which Gamow was allowed out of

14. G. Gamow letter to the author, 6 Nov. 1967. This account is repeated, with some minor variations (for Gamow was a great storyteller), in his "Getaway from Russia," a typed four-page autobiographical sketch, dated 13 Oct. 1950, in the Gamow collection, Library of Congress, Washington, D.C., and in his published autobiography, *My World Line* (New York: Viking, 1970), pp. 91–133.

15. *My World Line.*

16. *Last News* (Paris), 9 Mar. 1935.

Russia. Moreover, it is questionable that the Soviets would have considered Kapitza a realistic hostage for Gamow's return. And, finally, because Gamow registered at the Russian Embassy upon his arrival in Washington, D.C., where he had a visiting professorship during the 1934–35 academic year, and announced his formal intention to remain in the United States only some time *after* he was made aware of Kapitza's plight, it seems that the Kremlin officials could only have guessed at Gamow's plans at the time they made their decision to limit Kapitza's freedom.

Yet, the Moscow authorities might well have been suspicious of Gamow by this time, for it was a year after the Solvay Conference he attended, and word of his discussions with Bohr, Langevin, and Curie must have filtered eastward. This word may, in fact, have traveled eastward by first class mail, for Kapitza believed that his own difficulties stemmed in part from Gamow's request to Vyacheslav Molotov, Chairman of the USSR Council of Ministers, that he be granted the same promise of free return to Western Europe or America that Kapitza had had.[17]

Such individual problems, however, were merely symptoms of the widespread and profound crisis affecting all traditional Russian science. This science had been little changed during the first decade of Soviet rule. But with the formulation of Five-Year Plans to industrialize and collectivize the Russian economy, science could no longer be a passive bystander; its services now were required by the State.

Before the Revolution, the level of Russian scientific activity was that of an "underdeveloped" country. For the same period, the same may be said of the United States. Just as America pointed with justifiable pride to Franklin, Henry, Gibbs, Rowland, and Michelson, Imperial Russia paid homage to Lomonosov, Lobachevsky, Chebychev, Lebedev, Butlerov, and Mendeleev. Yet, such outstanding scientists were few and far between and their contributions stood out all the more against the weak backgrounds of domestic scientific activity.

The world "center of gravity" of research and teaching in science clearly lay in Western Europe. There the strong tradition of such endeavors could be traced back to the great scientific revolution of the

17. Kapitza's statement of 19 Aug. 1935, recorded by E. D. Adrian.

seventeenth century. And it was there, especially to Germany and England, that students from such countries as America and Russia went for their advanced training. Not until the second quarter of the twentieth century did these two underdeveloped nations make their great leap forward, a leap which, in fact, took them both to world leadership. In the United States the transformation began with Americans returning from abroad with advanced degrees, progressed with numerous visits by eminent foreigners, and with the "schools" of theoretical and experimental physics established by Oppenheimer, Lawrence, and others, and was completed by the scientist-refugees expelled from Germany who contributed their skills to such wartime activities as the atomic bomb project and remained in the United States thereafter.[18]

The rise of Soviet science to the front rank parallels that of America in the features of training abroad, foreign visitors, and conscientious efforts to improve quality, but there were also other ingredients. Ideologically motivated, the government dictated the direction of research, while funding it handsomely. This financial support was welcomed by most of the leading scientists; the control was not. Whether Soviet science would have surpassed its present high level with greater individual freedom is an unanswerable question. Certainly the government would have been less generous were it not determined that science should be useful and therefore closely guided.

Upon assuming power the Bolsheviks recognized the shortage of scientifically and technically trained people in Russia. Indeed, for a party committed to the "construction of socialism" through a managed economy, far greater numbers would be required. Yet the specialists were largely unsympathetic, even hostile, to the new regime and this bourgeoisie was necessarily to be the teacher of the next generation of proletarian specialists, while its skills were indispensable until these more politically trustworthy replacements were educated. Faced with this dilemma the Bolsheviks proceeded cautiously. Scientific planning and organization made relatively little progress during the years of the New Economic Policy. Interference with the

18. Charles Weiner, "A new site for the seminar: the refugees and American physics in the thirties," *Perspectives in American History*, 2 (1968), 190–234.

freedom of scientific inquiry was limited. Even deviant political views were tolerated among scientists, as long as they did not act upon them and they continued their work.[19]

Not forgotten, however, was the ideologically inspired direction intended for Soviet science. All phases of intellectual development were considered part of a "social superstructure" by the Communist party theoreticians, a framework resting on the economic base of production. This superstructure customarily provided the dominant social class with ideological weapons which it used for its own purposes. In the Soviet Union these weapons were to be employed by the proletariat in the formation of the socialist society. The social sciences certainly were seen to be part of the superstructure: as early as 1913, Lenin remarked, "There can be no impartial social science in a society founded on class struggle."[20] By proximity and by analogy the natural sciences likewise were deemed appropriate tools for ideological purposes. In practice this meant that scientific objectivity fell victim when it appeared to be in conflict with the prevailing interpretation of Marxism-Leninism.[21]

And, of course, merged into the philosophical arguments were the Communist party desires that science aid materially in fashioning the new society. Service to the people was the highest goal; personal desires were secondary. Thus, despite inclinations to basic research, scientists should direct their work along socially beneficial paths. While the Marxist doctrine of the unity of theory and practice could be taken to imply that *all* research ultimately would prove useful, the emphasis nevertheless was placed upon work whose practical effects were quickly visible—a situation perfectly suitable to the industrializers. Applied research was regarded more favorably than basic re-

19. David Joravsky, "Soviet scientists and the great break," in Bernard Barber and Walter Hirsch, eds., *The Sociology of Science* (New York: Free Press of Glencoe, 1962), p. 112.

20. V. I. Lenin, *Collected Works*, vol. 16, p. 349, quoted by Lazar Volin, "Science and intellectual freedom in Russia," in Ruth C. Christman, ed., *Soviet Science, A Symposium Presented on December 27, 1951, at the Philadelphia Meeting of the American Association for the Advancement of Science* (Washington, D.C.: AAAS, 1952), p. 90.

21. Volin, "Science and intellectual freedom." Also see David Joravsky, *Soviet Marxism and Natural Science, 1917–1932* (New York: Columbia University Press, 1961).

search and was particularly promoted in fields such as petroleum geology and chemical engineering. In the program of creating a modern, self-sufficient state, resources had to be located and technical industries developed for their exploitation. Moreover, traditional Russian strength had been in theoretical, not applied, science, and rectification of the imbalance was felt to be desirable. Consequently, no government in history gave more encouragement to science and technology.[22] Leaders of the Soviet Union saw science not only as the key to Imperial Russia's physical problems but to its spiritual backwardness as well. By a single process the wealth of the land would be utilized *and* the age-old religious mysticism overcome. In Soviet scholar Loren Graham's terse phrase, "Science would modernize both Russia as a state of nature and Russia as a state of mind."[23]

How was this to come about? Through planning. In a country whose communist theorists wished to plan all spheres of human endeavor, especially economics, science was regarded as perfectly amenable to the process. But there were difficulties, for how does one go about planning discovery or the large intuitive component of theoretical science? During most of the 1920s the issue was sidestepped, as scientists were reassured that even their self-guided research, conceived without thought of social utility, nonetheless produced that utility. When, later, rigid controls were applied, the scientific administrators were far more successful in planning *for* research than planning *of* research.[24]

Given this interest in organization and planning, it may seem surprising that the Soviet Union's first Five-Year Plan (1928–32) specified no supreme body to oversee scientific programs. The explanation hinges strongly on the circumstance that there was no group of eminent and competent scientists who favored such a plan. The most prestigious scientists were members of the Academy of Sciences, and that organization was an anachronism in Soviet society, an un-

22. Loren Graham, *The Soviet Academy of Sciences and the Communist Party, 1927–1932* (Princeton: Princeton University Press, 1967), pp. 39–42, 78.
23. Ibid., p. 33.
24. Ibid., pp. 43–44, 64.

reformed czarist institution. Nearly a decade after the Revolution not a single academician was a member of the Communist party. The party understandably mistrusted the academy, a feeling warmly reciprocated as the academicians were skeptical of planning in science. In this situation the government could not proceed as it wished, for the academy, in its institutes, conducted the most advanced research in the country, all the more unique as research quality in the universities declined following the admission of hordes of unqualified proletarian students. The question slowly crystallized: Would the academy reform itself or would it be replaced as the leading scientific organization in the USSR?[25]

A counterpart Communist Academy had, indeed, been established earlier but the main thrust was aimed at transforming the Academy of Sciences. New charters imposed in 1927 and 1928 withdrew much autonomy previously held by the academicians. The membership limit was raised from 45 to 85, the Communist party and other organizations acquired the right to nominate candidates, new chairs were created in subjects likely to be pursued by Marxist scholars (e.g., socio-economic sciences, dialectical materialism), and places were reserved for engineers ("technological sciences") for the first time. Despite opposition, numerous Communist party candidates, including Bukharin, the prominent party theoretician and a leading advocate of planning in science, were thereby elected to the academy beginning in 1929. Some quickly assumed positions of influence, and within a few years the institution was effectively sovietized. As the academy controlled Soviet science far more than did similar societies in other countries, science on a national basis came under ideological domination.[26]

The academy did not succumb to these external pressures as easily as it may seem in this very brief summary. The battle over goals, organization, and operating policies in the nation's scientific research laboratories, as in the academy, was intense. Yet the outcome could hardly have been in doubt. Threats of arrest and violence against academicians were unnecessary; fear of expulsion from the academy was

25. Ibid., pp. 30–31, 77.
26. Ibid., pp. 86–87, 90, 114–15.

frightening enough. Members of other organizations involved in Communist party takeovers at this time were being purged, and this fact could not have been lost upon the leaders of Soviet science. By the end of 1929 more than one hundred academy employees had been arrested and more than five hundred fired. In the next two years the first several academicians (initially all were historians, i.e., social scientists) were arrested and most perished in prison camps. Relatively few fled abroad, and their professed motivation was personal rather than a belief that the pursuit of science required intellectual freedom. For those who remained it was a time to announce loyalty to the theory and practice of communism. They had been mildly treated during the first decade of Soviet rule, but in 1927 the government began to stage its famous show trials in which "bourgeois" technical experts were accused of "wrecking activities," that is, sabotage, and prosecutor Andrei Vyshinsky questioned whether the country could trust its specialists. By 1930 the terror had moved from engineers working on dams and electrical power plants to the hall of the Academy of Sciences.[27]

But specialists were not the only persons subjected to the terror. Indeed, it pervaded society. When Stalin chose to restructure the Soviet economy, massively and quickly, he determined also upon harsh means to this end. In the first Five-Year Plan collectivization of agriculture and rapid industrialization were emphasized. While farms were to be made more efficient by consolidation, the major goal was to transform the Soviet Union from an agricultural to an industrial nation. Consequently, the production of energy and construction materials was regarded as a necessary first step. Figures for coal, oil, electricity, steel, other metals, timber, cement, all increased dramatically. Heavy industry was again emphasized in the second Five-Year Plan (1932–37), at the expense of consumer goods, though greater attention than before was paid to efficiency of production and quality of the product. Although these plans may have been underfulfilled in certain areas, there is no question of their overall success: Russia became an industrial giant. Further, there is no doubt that the human toll was enormous. Aside from the resisting farmers, the purges, which reached their peak of intensity in the period

27. Ibid., pp. viii, 95, 120–21, 125, 129, 149, 176–77, 181–82, 185–89, 206.

1934–39, claimed millions of Soviet citizens, including the highest military and political leaders, diplomats, Communist party chieftains, two heads of the secret police, and scientists.[28]

When Kapitza began his forced residence in Russia his government had already begun to exhibit its ruthlessness toward its own people. Although natural scientists were purged far less frequently than their social scientist colleagues, and although Kapitza's special combination of scientific and engineering talent was understandably attractive to the Soviet leaders, his almost foolhardy, defiant courage is nevertheless impressive, as is the fact that he got away with it.

The reason for his "luck" must lie in the circumstance that he was not threatening to any person or goal. Were he involved in such controversy as surrounded Lysenko's destruction of genetics in the Soviet Union, which began about this time, he could well have been accused of political defects and been liquidated. Were Western pressures for his release as irritating as the protest election of Lysenko's chief opponent, N. I. Vavilov, as president of the International Congress of Genetics in 1939, or the angry resignation of many foreign members of the Soviet Academy of Sciences when Lysenko finally routed all his enemies in 1948, then Kapitza might have suffered Vavilov's fate: death in a prison camp.[29] But Kapitza stood not for a disputed scientific view or ideology; even the Soviets could find some value in the concept of internationalism in science. His desire to work in peace, in a place of his choice, was not the kind to engender strong opposition in the Soviet scientific community. Further, he was so newly on the scene that he threatened no vested interests. Jealousy of the largess offered him might have been grounds for initiating intrigues against him, but as the government wanted to be his sponsor, such schemes could backfire.

If the reason for Kapitza's detention was the practical desire to improve electrification of the nation, that project *was* progressing, and doing so without the kind of crises that plagued agriculture following collectivization and which permitted the rise of Lysenko. If the

---

28. J. N. Westwood, *Russia, 1917–1964* (New York: Harper & Row, 1966), pp. 89–92.

29. Zhores Medvedev, *The Rise and Fall of T. D. Lysenko* (Garden City, N.Y.: Doubleday, 1971), pp. 5–6, 8–10, 66, 134–35, 138–39.

rulers of the Kremlin kept Kapitza for the more long-range goal of elevating physics in the Soviet Union, that too could proceed without crises. So there was negligible domestic turmoil surrounding his envisioned career, and the bureaucrats, who seem to have had good intentions toward him, could calmly wait for him to cooperate, while the scientists could ignore him.

And yet—logical explanation of this situation cannot wholly overcome a sense of awe. Kapitza was a maverick in a country that did not tolerate deviation, a nation that devoured its creative sons, a state whose actions were often irrational. Despite the explanation, therefore, we must be impressed with his survival.

«« 4 »»

Letters from the Soviet Union

To keep Rutherford informed of her husband's actions and attitudes during the first year of his detention in Russia, Anna Kapitza excerpted portions of his letters to her and gave them to Rutherford. These are printed below.

9 November 1934
Leningrad

To me my position is quite clear, and I see that I can do only one thing. This is as I had written to you beforehand, to change over to bio-physics. A summary of arguments of my decision I am writing today. The question of the transfer of my laboratory, and more than that, the question of the building of the new one for work in low temperature and magnetism, these questions are over. You remember that in Cambridge I could not decide for a long time to build a laboratory, and the year it was being built and I was still working in the old one was not the happiest time of my life. It is torture for me and I only accept it as a sad necessity. In Russian conditions the building of the laboratory like mine will mean colossal administrative difficulties and will spoil my life. Over and above all, I am convinced that the difficulties are so great that, in any case, for me not experienced in all very complicated bureaucratic processes, it will be quite impossible to overcome them. You know how cross and worried I got and cursed at every misunderstanding we experienced with our car. . . . And the building and administration of a laboratory would be a continuous cursing and 99% chance that I should end in the lunatic asylum. I have no collaborators here and this is all the tragedy.

I believe fate itself sent me bio-physics to solve the difficulties. Of course they will be cross with me here for a time, but if it will be necessary I could prove it, I am sure, that it is the only domain in which I could work here. The fact is that to change the domain in physics itself I cannot. First of all I

Institute for Physical Problems, Moscow. Courtesy of Peter Kapitza.

am not interested in other parts of physics but the one I worked in, and all new, really new, work in physics is almost always connected with such highly developed technical installations which will again involve the solving of administrative questions. . . . Trying to restore my old work down here I should waste a lot of money, ruin myself and get at no useful purpose. And I should be messing alone in my room instead of parading as a director of a laboratory, as to that I have no ambition. Of course I do have ambition and I am not ashamed of that, but why everybody here thinks that it ought to be such a silly one?

At the end there is more happiness in a good discovery than in a smart study. Of course it is fine to have both as I had in Cambridge, but when I have to make my choice, without the slightest hesitation I choose the work.

[November–December 1934]
Leningrad

I saw several times Krjajanovsky.[1] He is an academician and the initiator of the electrification of the Union. . . . He knew of my work, but unfortu-

1. G. M. Krjajanovsky, also spelled Krzhizhanovsky, the leading communist power engineer, was elected to the Academy of Sciences in 1929, and to the aca-

nately from somebody in England or even Cambridge who told of it with many mistakes. All this is very stupid and very bad. You know often one misrepresents[2] scientific work, and some people even enjoy it as if they did it on purpose. I of course told him about my thoughts and ideas.

[November–December 1934]
Leningrad

They think that planting me here they can create science, if even in the part I am interested in. I feel I can be of much more use as a stimulator and a critic. And being the link between the Russian and English science. . . . If a socialist country can have trade relations with a capitalist one, why not the same in science? . . . The scheme of the transfer of my laboratory reminds me of the Arabian nights.[3]

[December 1934]
Leningrad

I know I shall have no strength to organise a laboratory here. . . . Everyone is promising and promising and nothing else.

26 December 1934
Leningrad

Without confidence[4] I cannot take on myself the responsibility of the transfer of the laboratory in one year's time. . . . I tell in my memorandum that I can only do pure science. This is the sense of my life, and without my

demy's Presidium, as a vice-president, the following year, in the big elections held with the "active participation of the Soviet public."

2. By "misrepresent," Kapitza meant describing his research as applicable to warfare. This note, and many following, are based upon Anna Kapitza's comments on her husband's letters, or her summaries thereof.

3. By this time the Soviet authorities must have reacted to Kapitza's strenuous assertions that the country's industrial capacity could not furnish the materials and equipment he required, and proposed, therefore, to purchase the contents of the Mond Laboratory.

4. The recurring question of "confidence" refers not to Kapitza's belief in his own abilities but to his government's trust in him. Confidence and trust, in situations not unlike Kapitza's, are favorably discussed—when he was out of office—by Nikita Khrushchev in *Khrushchev Remembers* (New York: Bantam, 1971), pp. 573–77.

laboratory I can do no work. I cannot build it again as this is impossible. Then the only way for them is to buy it and transport it. . . . This is possibly a "priority." . . . But I want to explain the need and the necessity of pure science and its internationalism. . . . Rutherford knows me better than anybody else.

[January 1935]
Moscow

Without doing anything in reality, the Academy already published about the new institute.[5] This is of course very touching and very characteristic for us; we always talk and do not.

[January 1935]
Moscow

If only I would be allowed to do the talking for the transfer of the laboratory, I am sure we could arrive to some settlement without any quarrel and disagreement. But now I do not want to take any part in it, not till I have 100% confidence; otherwise it is foolish. . . . Only now I understood what work meant to me. The loss of my scientific work I feel very acutely, and the pain is vivid. If I did not know it before, how people who know science only from the administrative point of view, how can they understand it? . . . I don't think anything could be done without me, and there is no understanding yet and I feel it is not coming by a long way.

[January 1935]
Moscow

Well, as about the level of the technical developments,[6] it is not high enough for making my helium liquefier. Of course, if one wants to develop several new branches of metal industry and also the machine building one, then it will be possible.[7]

5. Kapitza was shocked to learn of his nomination as director of the Institute for Physical Problems from the newspapers.
6. Kapitza had been inspecting certain aspects of Russian industry.
7. About this time he was astonished by the "coincidence" that there was a young communist named P. Kapitza, who wrote in the newspapers and got mixed up with him.

[January 1935]
Moscow

[My life condition is] like the one of the second rate foreign specialist who from fear of unemployment came here. . . . I shall not refuse any work, but is any of my creative work possible in such atmosphere of distrust? I doubt it. . . . If Maisky says I am happy it is an impudent lie. . . . Only seven days ago I wrote to Mezhlauk[8] that I am weary, that I lost interest in life. . . . I feel I had fulfilled the problem of acquainting myself with the conditions of work here, honestly. But if one wants to ascribe to me thoughts I have not got, against this I can do nothing.

[January 1935]
Moscow

I will stop all the work of the transfer of the laboratory and go to work with Pavlov.[9] I hope that I shall be allowed. . . . The most painful for me is to be without work. . . . It is so difficult to switch over to the Cambridge lab matters. I felt a vivid pain and all the nonsense of my position, and if I do not think about the science it is not so acute.[10]

[January 1935]
Moscow

I feel it more and more difficult to work in this atmosphere of distrust. It passes on everyone around. . . . I am quite alone. . . . Into physiology I shall

8. Valeri I. Mezhlauk was vice-chairman of the Council of Peoples' Commissars of the USSR and the Council of Labor and Defense, and chairman of the State Planning Commission of the USSR. Like many others, he was arrested in 1937 and executed the next year. Mezhlauk was the highest official with whom Kapitza had fairly frequent contact. For the first months of his detention, Kapitza stayed in Leningrad and, in fact, refused when asked to go to Moscow. "Professor," he was told, "you do not realize what you are saying. You cannot say no to a government order."

9. Kapitza seems to have had no training in physiology or any evident ability in this field but was probably drawn to it by Pavlov's experimental techniques, which required no elaborate apparatus, and by Pavlov's reputation as the only outspoken scientist who dared to criticize certain government actions.

10. About this time Kapitza wrote to his wife not to think of coming to Russia. He feared that she would not be let out again, and that if he were then permitted to go

go completely only after I shall be convinced that I can do nothing for our science in the main line of my knowledge. This is why I take every opportunity to show how and what has to be done to recreate my laboratory here. But as there is no confidence, my advices are taken not as I want them to be.

I think of what Maisky said and I am surprised you can take notice of it. He is a professional man and his profession puts on him certain obligations. At the end I shall talk too one day. I will not be silent always, but I do not want a quarrel. I always did such a lot to prevent people from quarreling, and especially people of science, so I am ready to sacrifice myself so the international relations will not suffer.

My everyday life you can see by what I ask you to send me, how it is arranged.[11] . . . [I could live very well if I chose to do all sorts of odd jobs, such as consultations to the cinema, etc., but,] unfortunately, then there will be no time left for scientific work. . . . They wanted to prove to me that one could create for me conditions in which I could work, but already two months passed and nothing was done.

[Joffé[12] asked me to join in the discussion on superconductivity in the next session of the Academy,] but this for me will be tortures of Tantalus. On this question I do not agree with many people and of course with Kharkov school which will take part in the discussion. My work in this field is in the mid way. Some results I have, but they are not yet verified. Of course I shall feel like Goliath with bound arms, and if we arrive to some conclusions after the discussion then Kharkov people can verify it and I will sit like a fool. It was wicked on Joffé's part to have asked me, and now my refusal can be interpreted very badly. To the devil with it. But here you have an example of Joffé's good will to me. On the surface it seems as if he specially cares for me, and at the same time it is difficult to believe that he does not really realize how painful it is to me to discuss scientific questions.

It comes to that all, as well here as abroad, will try that my work continues. This is the interest of all as science is the domain of all. And where and how we shall live, that concerns you and me. . . . I always wanted to work for the Union, but never the conditions were suitable. Now Mezhlauk says they are. I studied it and came to the conclusion that the conditions of life are bad and the technical base is also bad. . . . The only thing we know how to do is

---

abroad, she would have to remain as a hostage. Such a situation would have been intolerable, as it would have shown his government's lack of confidence in him.

11. He asked Anna to send everything from lavatory paper to trousers, and when the parcel arrived he was forced to pay a duty of about 3,000 rubles. A family of four, he noted, could live for a month on 1,000 rubles.

12. Abram Joffé, an eminent physicist, was Kapitza's former teacher.

build laboratories. . . . I am not kept in the course of conversation about the buying and transfer of the laboratory, but from the newspaper I know that the new laboratory will be attached to the Academy.[13]

[1 February 1935]
Moscow

I will talk to Mezhlauk, and as everything is promised on paper, and nothing really comes out of it, after two or three weeks of the same, I shall just go to Pavlov. When I was in Leningrad, we talked with him about the position of the scientists and he very correctly looks upon freedom, which is necessary to the scientist. With a stick one can only make the man dig in the ground and not to do scientific discoveries. He already wrote about it. The telephone stopped me; I am asked to the Kremlin to see Mezhlauk; I shall write about it when I shall come back.

2 February 1935
Moscow

Yesterday's talk with Mezhlauk was a very long one (2½ hours) and it was very important. Really, for the first time, I felt that they were interested in me as a man, and are really prepared to do everything to help me to start my work here. You shall be astonished, perhaps, that we least of all talked about everyday life and technical conditions. Mainly, and only, we discussed the question of confidence. This took a long time, and the fact that Mezhlauk looked upon it as seriously as I did, and did not want to pass over it lightly, but on the contrary considered every point of it separately, gave me a very good impression. I talked, usually freely, but not harshly. Mezhlauk gains everyone, and harsh words do not come to the lips. But the frankness was complete from my side, and I also felt it in many things that Mezhlauk said.

13. In many of his letters Kapitza stated that he could not begin work in Russia until the atmosphere of distrust and suspicion was gone, and he urged Rutherford not to come to any agreement with Maisky. He also commented that the cottage in the Crimea and a flat in Moscow were yet empty promises, but until his future was settled he did not want them. Such extra good living conditions would only make him more miserable due to colleagues' envy, and he would be more isolated, if that were possible. The press carried information of these fringe benefits when his detention was made public, e.g., *The Observer*, 28 Apr. 1935.

This conversation can be described as follows. There is no more distrust in me, that all that was is left behind and is explained. But if they do not want to give me complete freedom, it is only because they are afraid that after getting back to my old working surroundings, I shall not have enough courage to tear away from it. My arguments came to the following: if for 13 years, in spite of all the inconveniences, I was the son of my country, that in future I will do the same. But the time spent will not be lost. It is quite impossible by force to make a man known as I am to sit here. If our "characters" do not agree, and I shall not be "happy" here, nothing will make me stop here, and as it is impossible to guard the man for ever, my position will be that of the unstable equilibrium, from which it can always slip off. So they have to throw away all the methods of pressure and try to find a way out by which we all shall be satisfied. This is easy and simple. First, I have no feeling of anger or offense, because in times of such great and historical facts which are going on now it is silly and foolish to talk about personal offenses. Misunderstandings do always arise and can arise even greater, but one must liquidate them at once. Secondly, I want to help and to take part in the developments of science in the Union, and did already everything I could. I am certain that as soon as I shall have full confidence, I shall with ease arrange that in the shortest time I and my laboratory will be here. And after all, if I am not sincere, and only pretend to be friendly, then in any case nothing will come out of this. And so the only way is the first one. So you see everything is clear and simple. Of course, if they want to have some formal guarantees, I am quite prepared to accept them, but myself shall not produce them. I consider it degrading. I felt that Mezhlauk understood that one could talk to me as with a "good" one. That I really am the friend of the Union and that the main thing is to show that one really seriously cares for my scientific work here, seriously, and not only to justify the words of Maisky. Of course, Mezhlauk is not alone, and I would very much like to talk to his colleagues. I told him so. In any case we shall meet on the 14th. This conversation cheered me up and made my mood better, and it was pretty bad. Of course, I work here a little all the time and give consultations. If only my work were here I should be quite happy. Well, my memorandum is said to be interesting, even though I criticised a lot of things in it. What surprised me is that I was the only scientist who, by his own initiative, went to see the factories, so Mezhlauk said to me. That is why they were all so nice to me there. I had your 67 letter.[14] It is very good that you write about things so openly; go on doing it. Do not worry Rutherford, I love him dearly.

Yes, Maisky, by your letter, cannot get a prize for brains. P.S. We all at the

14. Both Peter and Anna numbered their letters.

moment are taken by the change of the Soviet constitution.[15] Well done!
How many vicious mouths will be shut by it. Do send me cuttings with the
comments. The impression must be terrific in Western Europe.

5 February 1935
Moscow

But if I shall have to sit another week or so, and as I have actually nothing
to do, I cannot see how one cannot let me go to Pavlov to work.

Now I want to write more fully about "O."[16] He is, of course, "non
arian," small, energetic and even educated; he finished the faculty of economics. He was Director of the Institute of Aluminium and afterwards the
optical one; now he must arrange the transfer and starting of my laboratory.
He has little work at the moment, and he still works at the Optical Institute.
He is also supposed to look after my welfare, but this, as I understand, he
finds beneath his worth. He is not in the least modest and when he wants
something he tries all the means. So when I was critical about the flat he
tried to persuade me to the contrary at first by flattery and afterwards he
started to frighten me. You remember first Leipunsky[17] and Semenoff[18]
and now "O." But "O" did it much more rudely than the others. On the
whole it is really amusing, this system of "intimidation," as it only frightened
away all my so-called friends, and as far as I know they will be frightened of
me for a long time yet. It is a curious feeling to realise that one must not
come to them; after being friendly one comes to the feeling of fright. This is
the reason why I do not go to see Aunt Lisa. I talked to Mezhlauk, and he
pointed out that without confidence in me it will be quite impossible for me
to have normal relations with people. Of course the words of "O," to the ef-

15. The Seventh All-Union Congress of Soviets approved proposals for electoral reform that included secret ballots instead of a show of hands, direct election of higher
legislative and administrative officials, and equal representation per unit population
for urban and rural areas.

16. Possibly a man named Goldberg, whom the Western newspapers claimed was
his assistant director (*The Observer*, 28 Apr. 1935).

17. Alexander Leipunsky was a physicist on the staff of the Physico-Technical Institute of the Ukrainian Academy of Sciences, later director of its Physics Institute, and
still later a professor at the Moscow Engineering and Physics Institute. He worked in
the Cavendish Laboratory in 1934 and 1935.

18. Although Kapitza gives the initials as "A. K." in his letter of 25 July 1935, this
is probably N. N. Semenoff, the Nobel Prize-winning physical chemist elected to the
academy in 1932, who served as its vice-president in the late 1960s. Semenoff collabo-
rated with Kapitza on one of his earliest papers.

fect that it would be a pity if such a good scientist were to be shot, did sound a bit old fashioned to me.[19] As for his care about me, he does nothing and always gives excuses in being formally busy with cards, etc. His own affairs he arranges very well. Sometimes I feel very jealous as he has very good rooms in the "National" which are miles better than mine. "O" uses his "friends" very skillfully indeed. It is strange, but I am sure I am much more idealistically on the side of the present ideas and new construction than he is, and at the same time he is there to make them live. But he has good qualities; he is always very cheerful and his cheerfulness is very catching. So when I am sad, and nowadays I am often sad, I look at his impudence and cannot refrain from smiling. Then, he has no malice towards people. He is very cunning, cunning without limit, and I think he knows malice at the end always tells against oneself. So I think I need not await harm from him. I am, of course, very glad that this is only temporary, and he was nominated without *me* being asked about it. Here everybody does it, but I think this is wrong. Of course, even if I was asked about it, I had to give my consent, as all the people are alike before one gets to know them. At present I behave very calmly and very peacefully. But I do not despair that when such questions as confidence and buying of the laboratory, etc., will be cleared I shall make the same "O" work as I want to, and his energy can be used in the organisation of the scientific work. But always one comes to the same question of confidence; this is the centre of everything. Of course I saw it long ago, but here they begin to realise it too. . . . Do remember than even if I am sad I am still clever (in any case I think so).

20 February 1935
Moscow

To-day I am tired; it is thawing and this sudden change in the temperature always tells on my mood. The life is monotonous and dull. I feed in the Academy of Sciences restaurant. The food is eatable, but the place is too small and everything is badly organised. Much better organised is the restaurant of Semenoff in Lesnoe. At the moment the great event is the chess tournament. This is really an all-Moscow event. It has a lot of attention. The other event is the opening of the metro, this is going to happen in another few days.

19. Kapitza here shared the Western incredulity that such things could and did happen.

21 February 1935
Moscow

I interrupted the letter, my thoughts jumped and I did not know what to write. Today got your 77 letter. The parcel has not yet arrived. I shall wire the moment it will come so you could send the trousers and the rest. My darling, day and night I think of you and the children and of the present situation. I think in the next three weeks it must be decided if I go to work with Pavlov and quietly do bio-physics, or in earnest something will come out of the transfer of the laboratory. I cannot understand why Maisky did not talk to Rutherford. I was definitely told that it would be done.

You judge the situation very correctly, but if only you knew more it would make your arguments even sharper. Your characterization of "O" is very true, but you are more severe than is necessary. If he tried to intimidate me it only means that in his practice it gave positive results. Do you know "O" has a very good reputation here and they very sincerely value him quite a lot, and by giving "O" to me, at the same time a certain institute had been given a lesson. This is really what pains me most, how such completely unprincipled men like "O" can create themselves such a position. This only points to a completely unnatural relation between the scientists and the world surrounding them, if such "O" are necessary for their guidance and direction. Some day I shall write to you about the Academy; it is in an awful muddle. Our people do not know what to ask of it, and the others do not know what to do to gain affection and respect. From both sides they try very hard, but nothing comes out of it. It is most entertaining when the new building is discussed. Men of the elderly age picture themselves the building of the Academy as a temple of science, so the middle (the altar) is devoted, as for instance, to the earth, the aisles of the building to the animals, machines, etc. This is the plan of Fersman;[20] he is a geologist. Krjajanovsky also wants a temple, but in the middle he insists on "energy" (he is an engineer). Bach[21] puts the presidium and the library in the altar; this is a little better, to enumerate all is simply difficult. Let us suppose I have to build a factory, shall we say a brick-making one, or a mechanical ship. I can make a plan and it will be easy to criticise it, as everybody knows how a brick or a mechanical factory works. And nobody knows how an Academy works and what it produces and even what part it takes in the socialist construction. How after this

20. A. E. Fersman, a geochemist and mineralogist.
21. A. N. Bach, or Bakh, a chemist, was a Communist party member who, with Krjajanovsky and several other scientists, was in 1937 elected a deputy of the Supreme Soviet.

can one build a factory of pure science, if no one knows of this production? And at the same time everyone knows that scientists and science are necessary to the country. This is more an intuitive feeling, and sincere too, but these thoughts did not acquire a definite shape. I read the stenographical reports of the 17th party conference, and also almost all the speeches of the Soviet conference, and nothing was said about pure science. About applied yes, and nothing about pure (I wrote about it to Mezhlauk, but have not yet had a reply). And we find in the other historical occasions of the reconstruction of the state it was tried; as for instance, Peter imported scientists from abroad and created the Academy. Napoleon accompanied Laplace, etc., and altogether was encouraging science, and in his time French physics started to flourish, not like nowadays when France has almost no science. We also have a drawing towards science, but for the present the results do not justify the efforts in the domain of pure science. One says that when Molotov received the academicians (I was not present, of course) he said that the Academy will have unlimited help if they can present a clear and intelligent programme and plan. I am afraid in this manner the Academy will not get very much, but at the end it is not their fault, as they were not definitely told what they are supposed to give instead. I myself think that it is completely wrong to plan the production the part of which nobody seems to understand. Nobody has a clear idea of how science will join in the socialist reconstruction. This does not happen because there is no room for science in the socialist state; on the contrary the place will be a most grand one, but because the time is not ripe. All the efforts are now directed to the accumulation of the material basis on which the socialist society will be built. This accumulation is going on at a terrific pace, at such a pace that nobody could predict. But it is going so smoothly because its base is imitation; the country spends almost nothing on the creation of new technical forms. Research is all directed to the solution of different secrets and the mastering of different processes of general character which are very well known and mastered in Western Europe. For this work one does not require any special depth of thought or qualification, but the results are very spectacular, and the country indeed grows at the devilish pace. How long this phase will continue I cannot say, but it is clear that the position of pure science, if not completely nil, is not far from it. The scientist, let us take Pavlov, is considered a museum piece of which great care is certainly taken, and of which one is proud. For everyone it is clear that if tomorrow Pavlov and all his school will disappear it will certainly be a great pity, but it will have no effect on the life of the country and the main figures of the state planning department will not change. Not only Pavlov, but the whole of the Academy in its purely scientific part is not bound to the life of the country and if it all disappeared nothing will at the moment affect the planning, because at the moment there is no room for it in the active part of the life. In the coarse imitative period there is nothing to do for the indeterminate and searching mind. From this all the tragedy; they do not know what to ask from him and he does not know what to give. And the best the Academy can do to justify its existence is the mystical fear before science. They want to build for themselves a temple, are transporting poor Karpinsky[22] like a life relic in a 12 cylinder Lincoln. The position is tragico-comical; one destroys the cathedral of the saviour by the Moscow river to build another one by the Kalooga Gate.

I am certain when we shall enter in our socialist development into the period of original thought, then all will completely change. After collecting a sufficient material basis the industry organised on the socialist base will want not only to overtake the capitalist economy, but will go by its original paths; this is already noticeable now. Then the inventive mind and creation will have freedom in front of it; originality of mind will then be valued more highly than organising gifts, as is the present position. Pure science as the lever for knowledge of the surrounding nature, the domain for the most original way of thought and at last the most perfect method of the criticism will no doubt be the principal factor of the country's progress. Academicians carefully selected from scientists, and free from the cares of everyday life, will then tell without effort what Academy they require to give most productive work and to be the guiding star of the scientific life of the country. I picture myself the academicians young and gay, and the building of the Academy as a collection of business institutes, healthy and business like, built for the requirements and the needs of every scientist and just as easily destroyed and replaced by others when need might be. And the temple which is going to be built in the future will be considered only as a tombstone to the spirit of the old Academy, which is alas revered even now by the leading men of our country.

What concrete deduction do I make out of all this? First, a real place science has not got in the country. Secondly, as soon as the country is firmly established, science will then be the leader. But when it will all happen? As all the rest in life, it will happen gradually. If there will be war everything will be delayed, but I think at the end of the second five years our science will get well advanced. What ought the scientists to do now? One must train oneself to the leading part and not let any occasion pass when pure science can be developed and not to be upset by the temporary fear from the reconstruction. Our builders of socialism must reconcile themselves with a temporary

22. A. P. Karpinsky, a geologist, was president of the Academy of Sciences from 1917 to 1936.

breach between pure science and life, as all interference will only deteriorate the true face of science. Let life itself develop the tie between them, and then the face of the Academy from the outside, as well as from the inside, will be found by itself. The Academy must and will find its place. For the moment only one thing is necessary and that is not to let the scientists forget that they are part of the country where there is, at the moment, a colossal reconstruction, and very soon they will be asked to take the leading part in it. Do you see to what heresy I arrived? At present I picture the Academy as a society of young, gifted and modern scientists, put together to be trained in the spirit of the time, without being asked anything in return. The building of temples will only turn our scientists into priests who will fool the devotees, as many already do with success, even now. I am talking too much; it is 3 a.m. I did not want to write so much about the Academy, and you might not be interested. But when one has no one to speak to, one wants to say what one thinks. And in this I am almost certain I am not mistaken, but, alas, I feel that my point of view does sound paradoxical, even if it may at the end be true. And the live relics of Karpinsky will be replaced by some other live relics; the Academy is full of them. I shall not be surprised if the Academy of which I am dreaming, and which without doubt will be required by life, will be created independently and by itself. Life will show, and perhaps even soon.

Well now about the flat. I saw one more; it was a little better than the first one; it is of the type of Aunt Lisa's; an engineer lives there, and he is going to the factory. I see now that the moment when we have to come to live here we shall be given something. It will be about the third of what we have in Cambridge, but it is of no importance; we shall pull through. The principle is, of course, the basic question *of confidence*, and the organisation of scientific work. And with this everything is wrong. I really do not know what to do. Except for Mezhlauk, nobody speaks to me, and I feel completely cut off from everyone. The only person who shows interest in me is Shoora; she is a nice creature, and is very kind, but she has no wide interests in life and science. The academicians shrink from talking about the Academy. Your father only curses, but he, too, does not know what he wants. Never in my life was I so *lonely* as I am now. I feel my complete uselessness. Since my visit to the factories I have absolutely nothing to do. I did not refuse any work. I was quite ready to take part in the reconstruction of the Academy, but I was not asked.[23] Just one or two consultations, and that is all—absurd use of a

---

23. No doubt the academy, which moved from Leningrad to Moscow in 1934, had sufficient work without Kapitza's suggestions for change. Still, he seems to have been told by someone, perhaps Mezhlauk, that he was to be consulted on the changes to be written into the academy's new charter, which was adopted in November 1935.

man! If this goes on for another few weeks, I shall send everyone to the devil and go to work with Pavlov. There I shall have enough room in a corner of the laboratory, and I shall be happier than here with the impossible perspectives. The only things which are well arranged here for me are theatre tickets and cars. I cannot complain about it, and all this I owe to Mezhlauk directly and not to "O." The theatre is the principal support for me.

23 February 1935
Moscow

I received your 78 letter, and was very pleased with it. I was touched by the care of Rutherford; he was always very kind to me. Yes, the people in Cambridge spoiled me for the last few years with their care and their attention, so the attitude of the people here is more bitterly noticeable. Never before was I so badly treated. But I think they don't do it maliciously, but by stupidity, and also because they do not know differently, and mainly because, as I wrote to you before, we have no respect and understanding of the importance of the pure science. But all these are general considerations. And now, of course, I feel so much your care and the words that my friends think of me and love me. *NEVER* in my life was I feeling myself so *ALONE* as I feel now. Not only the colleagues of Mezhlauk, but no one who is busy building the country, does talk to me. The Academy of Sciences does not ask me to help in the organisation, as was decided at the beginning, as it seems from fear that something bad might happen. Krjajanovsky, who at the beginning talked with me about some questions of the organisation of education, etc., and who was willing to continue, also does not call me. And all my so-called comrades, the scientists, also do not want me. But I don't want either to see them, as all their questions on all most general subjects are very unpleasant to me. And in Cambridge I had to avert the stream of people who wanted to talk to me. I feel myself completely useless, and without work it makes me lose faith in my strength. It seemed to me that I was a good scientist and with public spirit. Even in Cambridge I left a mark. Take the club which it is the custom to connect with my name, of which, like old Pickwick, I was a permanent president. I think it will stay a long time. But dear, however sad and troubled I am sometimes, I understand that I must let myself go. I do everything so my nerves will be in order. I must admit that I have a bottle of Valerian, but nowadays I do not touch it very often. Specially I try to walk every day; the theatre also helps; I try not to concentrate on unpleasant subjects, etc. But now and again it hurts me to tears that it seemed I did everything for ours here. One cannot blame me for anything; not only I have sincere loyalty, but a deep faith in the success of the new construction. It seemed to me that here they must have been proud of my scientific success and of my behaviour, and the result is that they treat me like the dog's dung which they try to mould in their own way. This is only stupidity, stupidity, and nothing else; otherwise I cannot explain why Maisky is silent, and other things. As for instance, it is two months ago that started the preliminary work of the transfer of the institute. And nothing was done in these two months, but that I inspected the industry and made a list of the necessary equipment (except the one in Cambridge) and the plans of the laboratory. All this was done by me in a fortnight. It is ridiculous to look at "O" who is struggling with papers and the bureaucrats. What in England is done by a telephone call, here requires hundreds of papers. You are trusted in nothing. Even they do not believe you when you give your own address; a paper from the house committee is required. People here do not trust each other at all. Only trust the paper; this is the reason why it is such a scarce article! The bureaucratism is strangling everyone. Is strangling Mezhlauk also, who is often himself lost, and his orders are broken, diluted and destroyed in the paper stream.

Yesterday, to my great joy, your parcel arrived. All my clothes are completely worn out, and so it is very welcome. But do not think it is an easy job to get it. The duty on it is more than 1,000 rubles, so two of these parcels will take away my monthly earnings. It is clear that I cannot pay the duty and "O" said he will try to get it for me free of duty. The question is clear and simple. My pants are worn out, my shoes are worn out, these articles are not at the shop to which I am attached, so one must be only too glad you can send them to me. And at the same time I am a useful man (so I was told). I cannot go about without pants and cannot run at the shops; in any case would not be able if I have to work on science. Well, one must produce endless papers, have I or not imported by regulation, etc., etc. And when I shall get the parcel no one knows. But I am sure I shall get it. This bureaucratic apparatus has one quality, this is it really works. I mean if you have enough patience and skill, then you can succeed in obtaining what you want. On this men like "O" do their careers. If not for this apparatus three quarters of the population of Moscow would be unemployed; what an awful thing for the Moscow people. To destroy this bureaucratism will not be easier than it was to reform the village. One hopes it will be destroyed, but it is not an easy task. But if one mastered the village, why will one not master the bureaucratism? The people are holding at it, feeding on it. The bureaucrat is the parasite of our government. But he is not untouchable. There are in the Union such organisations which at the main get over the difficulties of the bureaucratic apparatus; one only wishes that their economic experience should be spread all over the country. Why this is not done, I don't know. As far as I can see, this is more the question of education than of organisation, and to educate takes years. But even after all the cursing on my part, I do believe that the country will come out of all these difficulties victorious. Believe that it will be proved that the socialist method of economy is not only the most rational one, but will create a state which will answer to all the best wishes of the world's spirit and people's ethics. But in its birth pains, for me as a scientist, it is difficult to find a place, as far as I can see, and I wrote about it in the last letter. The time is not yet ripe and this is the tragedy of my position. The only way out is to be placed under special care of the government. To be like a hot house plant. But is this right? Can I risk it? Is it not better to wait with it all? There are lots of things which are not clear to me. But life will show. . . . Your love gives me the power of life. I wish I could see the children, but all comes in succession.

P.S. Difficulties with the parcel. Writing to Mezhlauk; he does not answer ordinary letters, so this will be an extra nice one. I got the catalogues.

5 April 1935
Moscow

Leipunsky came yesterday evening; we talked with him for an hour and a half. He saw Mezhlauk and tried to persuade me in all sorts of impossible things. He got entangled in his own arguments, struggled helplessly, and was ashamed of his position. Of course my arguments are so logical and so well-finished that against them to speak is senseless. Without confidence it is impossible to work. Why one should have confidence in me in a year or a year and a half, when I all these 14 years never did anything which could break the confidence in me? Nothing can be brought against me? And not only I did not break the confidence in me, but did all possible for the Union and its construction. And there abroad it is more difficult to be true to the Union than here. Well, why then for all my good conduct, I am not only not thanked but they abuse me, accuse me of ridiculous things and completely wore me out? Leipunsky could answer nothing to it. "This is what they think and this is what ought to be done," was his only argument. We parted very drily; he came to me not like a friend but an emissary.

Yes, Mezhlauk does not want to see me, but now it is no more necessary. All is said and all is clear. Perhaps I shall try to talk to his elder colleagues, or write to them. This I had not yet decided. I do not see any point in it. It is so difficult to say about oneself: "I am an honest man, a good scientist. I am used to be treated like one. I think I rendered service to humanity and this gives me certain rights in life."

8 April 1935
Moscow

Here all is the same. My mood is a little better and I am proud that I do not let myself go and am not losing my courage. My position reminds me of my moral condition in which I was 16 years ago, when I lost my wife[24] and two children. I was then very troubled, the same apathy and no wish to live. But I was saved by deliberately not letting myself think about the past. I put away all the letters from my wife, did not go to the cemetery, hid all her portraits, in one word all that could make me remember the past. And you know even now I have not enough courage to read our old letters. The same I do now. All that reminds me of my laboratory, the thread of my thoughts which was cut, I avoid. This is why it is easy for me to study physiology, organical chemistry, bio-chemistry. But on physics, till my laboratory will be here, one must put a cross. An amazing situation I never thought I shall be put in it.

As to the institute all is in the state of projects. It seems that not only from Mezhlauk's side, but altogether, the interest in it is lost. I shall not be surprised if it comes to "O."

"O" is seedy, it is difficult for him, they don't give funds and supply with bad helpers. He himself says they are no more interested. This is because the ridiculous colours in which it was all painted disappeared, and because of which all this business started. And in pure science no one is interested here. I am almost certain that even if it all will be built and purchased from Cambridge (honeur oblige), in such atmosphere it cannot live. I shall be accused that I don't want to do it or something of the sort. The most sensible for me is to seek refuge in bio-physics. First, there my gifts are unknown, there is no scale to compare with my past scientific career, and secondly, there is no need in a complicated technical basis, which is necessary for my work and is now in Cambridge, and which is only possible to create if I shall be put in exceptional conditions. You know it is most amazing how the attitude changed. As for instance Mezhlauk, who wanted to receive me twice a month on the 2nd and 14th, receives me once in a month and a half and even then one must during a whole week telephone, and get an answer, perhaps tomorrow, wanted today but something arose which prevented, etc. No one shows interest in my paper on pure science except you. And only you are an important person to me.

Of course I did swear a bit, but who would take any notice of it if they really would think that I was an important scientist, and my work was needed by the country. Very characteristic is the incident with the parcel. Of course everyone understands that I came not intending to stay here and so did

24. This was Kapitza's first wife, Nadejda Tschernosvitova.

not take any clothing with me. It is quite natural for you to send me my underwear, which was almost all already worn. And to take duty, of course it also can be done, but if the duty is equal to my one and a half monthly wage, then of course it very seriously tells on my living, and I only can be glad that hurts me and not you (I still pay for the duty in installments). Well, I asked that the New Statesman should be allowed and it was refused. In one word it is difficult to imagine the attitude of less attention. My costume after 7 months begins to wear out, my shoes are completely torn (the ones you had sent I wear in the theatre); here they don't make them in chevreau. Why not let mine from England? "Not allowed and won't let in." A most "delicate" attitude to the Royal Society Professor once a prominent scientist.

But you know it is funny, all this really does not touch me very much. I do not feel all these privations. Either they are compensated by the pleasure of the theatre, which I get in the evening, or perhaps the love of comfort is only an acquired habit and by nature I am very simple. If I write about it and am interested in it, this is because it is a good test of the attitude towards me.

The possibilities of the great future can be judged by the details of the present. If in all these details there is no attention, in the big things of course there will be none. It is not nice to boast, but it seems to me that I am not without some clairvoyance, when from the beginning I decided to go over to physiology. Then it was looked upon as a kind of demonstration, and now the logic of life sends me in it, logic which in a month or two will be understood and clear to all. So you see on the main I have rather a happy nature. I can take a problem in any domain, only let it interest me, and I am not afraid to go over from physics to bio-physics, because in the present conditions I prefer a corner in Pavlov's institute than an institute of my own. Very possible that I am the only scientist in the Union with such feeling and my psychology is completely incomprehensible here. But the cause of it is very simple: the only thing which could make me wish to have my own institute 1) is the real development of my old work, and I am almost certain it will not be possible, 2) personal ambition, of course like everybody else I got, but in this direction it was fully satisfied when the laboratory in Cambridge was built for me. This is more "exclusive" than anything else in the same direction. It seems to me that in physics I left a mark and I can now change over to another domain. To work with Pavlov, who is such a great man, must be a great pleasure.

The only thing which pains me when I am in Leningrad, it is that your letters get there 3 or 4 days later. I do not feel myself so near to you as here. But living with your father or my mother I will lead a more normal life than in the Metropole. In any case I cannot see what can be raised against my going. About this I shall talk with Mezhlauk. I hope he will receive me sometimes. First they said that I must be here because I shall work in the Academy. But the Academy did not show any wish to take advantage of my experience and knowledge, and there is no proof to show that it will be done in future. Secondly, for consultations not more than twice a week I can come. And then as soon as the plans of the Institute will be ready, even without taking any notice will England sell the laboratory or not, there is nothing for me to do. The position is clear and simple.

Well dear, what a long letter I wrote to you. It is such a pleasure to talk to you; there is no one except you. Now I must go to the Ac. of Sci. I spend there an hour and a half a day, and even this is too much. I am in everything and directing all. I begin to think I am not a bad administrator. I do not spend much time, and all goes well. There is no fuss. I know all the main things and look in the details only when they show the character of this or that worker, as I must know the capacity of everyone.

Give my regards to Rutherford. He is very good, and how nice it would be if he could come here, as I cannot to him, but the old man must not take such troubles. He probably went to Brighton to play golf.

9 April 1935
Moscow

Yes it is very painful without work, painful that you are not believed, even when I tried to do everything, everything to tell the people: "I willingly forgive all the offenses which you made me suffer, all the injustice, etc. You see I try to do everything to help you in the creation of science. Why then this rude and senseless attitude and mistrust?" If I am as I am and not good enough, why keep me? There is a place where I am appreciated as a scientist. Very distressing and incomprehensible. I am still waiting for a talk with Mezhlauk and then will ask for an audience with M.[25] They wore me out completely. And specially complete undervalue of good attitude and good will.

To-day came Talmud from Leningrad; he is a very pleasant companion. Even if you do call him a hypnotiser, he is a very pleasant and kind hypnotiser. It was very pleasant to be with him.

11 April 1935
Moscow

My cold has gone. I got your 103 letter. Yesterday all the morning I was with Talmud. For two hours we discussed how one could rationally change the human clothing. From idleness what one does not do. After, looked

25. Molotov.

through the plans. I do not approve them at all. Then I went to the Ac. of Sci. "O" begins to be insolent again. Altogether all is beginning to be dreadful and without issue. Of course with such people and in such conditions there is no use to expect that in not only a year but in three, no work can be renewed. This is all, of course, because of complete disappearance of all interest in my work or myself. I sent you cuttings from the newspaper, without any comments so you could yourself feel the spirit and the atmosphere. Your remarks are quite right. The position is oppressing. The interest in my work disappeared, but on the other side the comrades-scientists were so alarmed that, even though on words one tried to put my work in conditions which plainly one only could call normal, they started without any constraint to be indignant. "If we shall have the same, we shall do better than Kapitza." Of course it is all nonsense, but with envy, suspicion, etc., the atmosphere is unbearable and dreadful. Fit for the theatre "Grand Guignol." I am afraid that all this is confused by Mezhlauk. He did not understand either my mentality or the surrounding people. In any case this problem is more difficult than in the beginning. I personally see only one issue, to retire quietly into bio-physics. I am still waiting the long-time-ago promised audience, but unfortunately it is off for a long time. Mezhlauk is ill again and is away from Moscow. And I must officially ask permission for my return to Leningrad.

Well you see my dear wife, how sad are my affairs. I know my dear that time will solve all, but it is difficult to wait. The present position is useless to everybody. Let us discuss: the scientists here are definitely opposed to my transfer here. "There he enjoyed himself while here we experienced all sort of privations, and now he comes and wants to be a boss!" This is why such cold attitude of the Academy and complete unwillingness to underline my transfer here. As if one has just taken one more porter to open the doors. Of course once my work is understood, and after finding out that all is purely scientific, they do not see any use in me. But even if now they are not pleased themselves that they started all the trouble, there is the prestige, and for this reason it is all formally supported, but I do not see. . . .

12 April 1935
Moscow

Someone came in and I interrupted the letter, to-day is the free day and I shall finish it. There are no letters from you and it is so sad. Well, I continue the interrupted thought. The situation is such that I feel myself a useless and foreign element. This feeling certainly does not help the development of my scientific work in the country. I am in an impasse from where I can see only one issue, to get off the scene, and to go in the new domain where I am a new man, where I must build everything from the beginning. I know it is difficult to begin a new way in the 40th year of life, but it is not impossible. But it seems to me more and more that it is 1000 times easier than to recreate my old work here. Then perhaps the comrades-scientists would be convinced that I do not want to be a boss, that all I want is to have science in the Union. And if they all have such ill feelings towards me it is only happiness for me to go in such modest corner. On the other side my refusal to take all the earthly goods will only underline the sincerity of my decision. Before going to Moscow, when I tried to go in physiology, it was interpreted as a demonstration (all nonsense but it was difficult to prove the opposite). Now after 4 months in Moscow, when almost nothing is done, all the weakness of my position in which I am now is clearly shown. Now when for all it is clear that not only I shall not be able to continue my work in physics, but even cannot join in the social scientific life. The Academy has its own honour and it will not allow, without its permission, to be put at its head a scientist even with a European name. Its prerogative is the choice of scientists. And all that the Academy does is to clear its position and on no account to show that Kapitza is a scientist who can be treated with respect. I do not care a scrap about it all, and I do not blame them, as I understand very well their mentality and also I recognise that every organisation, even though so structurally rotten as is the Academy, has the right to protest at the least sign of an attempt on its opinion. All this I saw clearly a long time ago, but to demonstrate to the others one needed time and example. Now they exist. The question is, is it convincing? I am not quite sure in it, but to have further proofs is difficult. Of course the question of self respect is a very sharp one. "How can it be that there is something we cannot do; nonsense we can do everything." This is true, if one wished one can do everything, but more difficult is the problem greater must be the wish. And all the tragedy is not that one cannot do it, but that the wish is not strong enough. The problem of pure science is not felt by the country. With every day, month, year, this wish is growing and some day it will be great enough to do what is necessary for the creation of science. But at the moment this wish is not big enough and this is why nothing is done. I wrote a paper about pure science; it was not noticed. They only said, why Kapitza tackles such problems? Here he is a new one in our country and he is appearing in a part of a reformer. Of course this is a characteristic exclamation for the present time! If really the country needed pure science, then it would be discussed everywhere and then the only thing for me to do will be to join in it. But it does not exist; all the scientists are frightened of it. And they are alarmed because their conscience is not clear. You probably understand the mentality of scientists. From one part, if he is an honest scientist, he wants the solitude in his work, individuality. From the other side, he wants acknowledgment and for this he needs organisations like the Academy of Sciences, with its titles, periodicals, meetings. A dishonest scientist also is frightened of too much order and planning in science, because his insolvency will be too apparent. So [through?] individualism and charlatanism (I wrote to you that we have it a lot) they resent organisation of science. And the generally condescending attitude which now exists from the part of the Government is quite approved by the scientists. They are looked after better than others. In their business no one understands a scrap, and it is so pleasant for the scientist to puddle in the disorder. Of course this is only possible because in the imitative period the country does not need *real* science. The country is developing on the account of Western science and so they need the scientists-interpreters and not original creators. And no one in the Government can understand if the man himself invented something or read in the foreign paper. And it is just the same how the man got his knowledge, but the important thing is how he will apply it for the growth and development of the country. This is valued. For this of course there is no need in an organised science. Of course even without the laboratory I can be useful to the country and I am doing it now. But to create an organised science, with which original scientific work is only possible, is not in the interest either of the scientists or the country. This is why there is no wish which could create the necessary conditions for my work in the country.

Talmud brought me coloured reproductions of the Schookin collection, so on my walls are hanging Degas, Cézanne, Picasso, Gauguin, and Manet. So the room is brighter. To-day is the free day, so I am going for a walk. I have now some friends who spend their time with me with pleasure. One of them is a writer and critic, rather well known. He is rather a muddle-headed intellectual, but nice fellow. His wife is beautiful, but as someone said about her, she is charmingly stupid.

My mood is better after I quarreled with Mezhlauk. I feel more energetic, and even if the senselessness of my position is the same, I somehow feel that it is not completely without hope in the world.

Yesterday I went to see a play of Prof. Skutarevsky, adapted from the story of Ionov. Mezhlauk advised me to go. I shall write about it in the next letter. It is amusing to see how "the public" imagines themselves professors and science.

13 April 1935
Moscow

My dear, I want to write to you again, as often as possible. As it was before, my state of mind is rather bad, and only talking to you I can find some rest. Yesterday I went with Shoora to the Theatre to see the "Snow Maiden," and this also gave me some pleasure (of course not Shoora but the opera). I listened to this opera for the first time, but I knew a lot of tunes before. It gave me pleasure even if I don't always like Rimsky, but it was possible to get some rest. Here they say that to go to the Big Theatre is bad taste. As the Big Theatre belongs to the State, of course it is not very advanced, and it has the routine and classicism, which in its greater part is foreign to our spirit. It is true the production is very magnificent and it greatly pleases the provincials and the intourists. One day I took Kalinine. Do you remember my old mathematical master? He was very pleased and it was the first time in his life that he went to the Big Theatre. Afterwards I asked him to supper in the Metropole and we remembered the old time when he did not want to give me the full mark for my answers and work. In one word we enjoyed ourselves.

Yes dear, it is all like this, but my life is so empty now. Sometimes I rage and I want to tear my hair and scream. With my ideas, with my apparatus in my laboratory others live and work. And here I sit all alone; what for? I do not understand. I want to scream and break furniture. I sometimes think I begin to get mad. Only Valerian drops (mother's prescription) save me.

Yes my dear, the logic of your letters kills me, as you do not want to see the psychology or, better, mentality. Life is moved not by logic, but by emotions. You my dear, try to feel how I suffer sometimes; except for you no one cares about it. Do soothe me I implore!

Excuse dear the hysterics in the letters. It is inevitable and you must know, even if slightly, in what mood I am. For me it is quite clear now how one kills great men, how rude can the life be, and how difficult is the life of scientists when there is no such man as Rutherford, and what scoundrel Joffé is.

Well now about my affairs. Mezhlauk, as if to irritate me, is ill again. He has angina and poisoning. When he will come back is unknown. All this delays my return to Leningrad, which had to be on the 15th and now I shall go about the 19-20th. Well for to-day it is enough writing. Tomorrow I shall continue the letter, and to-day my mood is frightfully bad. I am sorry but I even want to be cross with you, and it does not happen very often. But I often think that you do not understand me.

14 April 1935
Moscow

My dear . . . yesterday I wrote to you and I was in a very depressed state. To-day is better, but I shall send yesterday's letter as you must know how I live here, what I do and what I feel, and how I feel the present conditions.

Yesterday I went again to the theatre. This time to a Chinese one on tour here. The performance began so as to give opportunity of the artists of the Moscow theatres to attend it. It was a very select artistic and literary meeting indeed. The performance was very interesting. The principal actor was Dr. Mei-Lan Fan. He only plays women's parts and it makes him into a real woman, so you simply cannot believe that it is the man playing and not the woman. The greatest impression is achieved by his mimic, which is reached by the movements of hands, and he reaches effects which cannot be compared with anything in the theatre. I heard everywhere about this theatre and only most delighted opinions, and now I saw myself how interesting it is to watch it. I was so sorry dear you were not there. You probably would like it even more than I did.

To-day I expected a letter from you but it did not come. You do not write to me if all my letters arrive. I always number them. Probably because of the bad weather your letters are late now and take a week to come. This is very sad, as for me to get your letters is quite an outstanding joy. All else is as dull as to-day's weather. Now I have to go to the Academy. It bores me, but I fixed my departure to Leningrad for the 19-20th.

In Leningrad I shall do physiology, and altogether it will be pleasant to live with mother. I love your father also very tenderly. The perspective of the journey gives me courage and gives me happiness (a very wee one).

My head is very empty. Other times I like to imagine, think about impossible experiments, just for myself. Just some exercise for the brain and now it is quite empty. It seems to me I am now stupid or begin to be more stupid. Science is so far away and so foreign to me. It begins to seem that life is by itself and I am by myself, and it does not frighten me to disappear from life's arena. Well, as soon as I let myself go, I again begin on sad things.

3 May 1935
Moscow

Here I am again in Moscow. I arrived yesterday. Here, as in Leningrad, the weather is not like May, cold and unpleasant. But it is all quite the same to me what is happening around. Yesterday we walked with Talmud and to day came "O." He reported what was happening here, but as usual I have to be careful what he says, as he does not like accuracy in his stories. But my darling, I feel I cannot live like this any more. One must change all and it will change. If they will go on torturing me like this, then I shall land in the home for the nervous cases. At the moment I am waiting for a telephone call; one must tell me when Mezhlauk is going to see me. This does not mean I shall see him. But shall continue the letter as soon as all will clear up.

4 May 1935
Moscow

Yesterday Mezhlauk received me, towards the evening, so it was difficult to write to you after it. I got your 115 letter, where you write that all appeared in the press, after I saw Mezhlauk, so when he put in front of me the number of The Times with the letter of Rutherford, I was amazed. He also gave me a telegraph press review of all the newspapers. I felt that something like this did happen, as the foreign journalists rang up "O" while I was away in Leningrad. Mezhlauk attaches great importance to it all and great significance. They are agitated. But dear, our talk was not very pleasant. How can I say that I am happy here now, when I am in complete isolation? How can I say that it is not dreadfully painful without my work? But of course the question is very difficult. Anna dear, I really do not know what to do.

To-day Mezhlauk sent me the letter of Rutherford in The Times, and I read it very attentively. Dear, I am splitting my head, what to do, but in my condition of apathy, well, let be what will be, but let me in peace.

Why should I take part in all this? I asked Mezhlauk to bring me with Molotov. There was a time when people counted it as a pleasure to meet me, and here it is the opposite.

Mezhlauk says, hardly Molotov would like to speak with me, and pointed out that if he himself does talk to me, one must take it as a great honour, which don't have either Karpinsky or Volgin.[26] Altogether he says I must obey them if the people gave them the right to rule the country. I said I obey in all and all I was ordered. But some of the orders sound as if Beethoven was called and told to write the 4th symphony, by order. Of course Beethoven can conduct an orchestra by order, but would scarcely be willing to write a symphony by order, in any case good ones. So do I consult and obey all they ask me, but I can not begin creative work, and of course Rutherford is right that Kapitza "requires an atmosphere of complete mental tranquility." And after the talk with Mezhlauk I was laid down for two hours. With all the worldly goods one cannot feel oneself happy when one part of the population does not talk to me because it is afraid and the other part because it feels too important.

But of course all this does not make me shut my eyes on the colossal work which is being done. I do agree with the socialist ideas and count it as right that the right to govern must be in the hands of the people who work. And I do not have any divergency with Mezhlauk and his colleagues but in the

---

26. V. P. Volgin, a Marxist historian and permanent secretary of the Academy of Sciences, the real power in the organization.

question of science (internationalism and freedom) and the attitude to me. I said to Mezhlauk that here they must obey me as they understand nothing in science. Either they must drive me away or obey. This he did not like. Well Anna, probably it will stop at that. Rutherford will complain and all will finish.

Well, by the way, the attitude to me, except for such things as parcel (you remember the duty on my old things was equal to my 2 months' wage), prohibition to get forcign papers, etc., is above criticism. I am well served with cars, and soon it seems I shall have the right to drive myself the car, which will be ascribed to me. This I did not do for 8 months. They provide me well with tickets to the theatre, and take steps to arrange the flat. The guardian angels[27] went back to heaven so I do not see them any more and I can go to Leningrad or whatever place I want to in USSR quite freely, though it seems they prefer me to stay in Moscow. Well now, about your visit. Mezhlauk says he will arrange with pleasure for you to come for 2 or 3 weeks to help me to organise and promises that they will let you out again. I am worried about the children, my dear. The children are ill such a lot this year. And how to leave them? And I know that you do look well after them. Sereja by your description is a very good boy and I wish Andrew would be the same. Mother has shown me his story with the mouth and how he got into the beast's stomach. Did he dream about it?

Yes, the 1st of May I spent with Semenoff. He came on the eve to spend the night and we talked very well. And in the morning went to find the comrades in the demonstration. We wandered for 2 hours before finding them. The manifestation people were very jolly; lots of music, and at the interruption of the movement starting to dance straight away. The people are gay and full of energy and the wish to live. It does carry tremendous impression. In the midst of all these happy people I felt even more alone and unhappy. Why don't they want to trust me? Am I too great an individualist to mix with the people? But where is the issue?

I went with the manifestation. Talmud was there and some of Semenoff's and Joffé's pupils. Talked a bit with them. Then went home, had dinner and went to see Talmud. He is very kind to me. Later came Semenoff and we talked about Soviet science. The Academy is lifeless and rigid, the scientific institutes are full of second rate or even hundredth rate scientists and all this is not a very bright picture, and is asking for great reforms. Of course the issue is only one—the youth (let us say up to 40), they must unite and come out with constructional criticism. We could find 6-7 people who are young (the Junior Ac. of Sci.) and who want to creat science. But all this only plans.

27. The police agents who followed him about.

In the evening of the 1st I went to Moscow. Of course the car from the garage of the Academy was again late, and I almost lost the train. In the carriage were only three people; the train was empty; no one travels in the Union in the night of the 1st to 2nd May.

You know it was strange to read the letter of Rutherford in The Times. As if there is written about a different Kapitza, who was a scientist, and whose fate interests scientists throughout the world. And now Kapitza is tiny, silly and unhappy, dangling on a string as were dangling the little spiders with wire legs which were hanged on the Christmas tree. They keep me by the string and I dangle helplessly my feet, for nothing, and do not move from the spot. Well, what did I do in these 8 months? Nothing! And how empty is this time and no one wants to understand me.

You are a good little wife, and only because of your letters I live. . . . I was very happy with your sketches of the children and do send me more. I know for you this is only few minutes and for me such a pleasure. The ones you sent me are hanging on the wall and I do admire them often.

5 May 1935
Moscow

I was sitting in my bath and naked rushed to the telephone. It was the correspondent from the Observer. I asked to ring me again in 15 minutes. I hate correspondents and at the moment more than ever. I must go to the Academy. I must tell the presidium about my work in England. This is the first time I am speaking about my work. It will be very painful, but nothing to be done.

I hope that Mezhlauk will see me on the 14th as it was arranged, but never was done.

The correspondent from Observer rang up again. I refused to him any information and interview. To the devil with them. If one will get mixed up with them one might get in such a stew that it will not be very pleasant. Well, I must go to the lecture. Shall write again when will come back and shall send it off. You see I write every day and it seems to me it is very interesting for you to get it like a diary.

Just returned from the Academy. There I was fighting for a bit. In any case I had to put the question freely, threaten to resign and all ended well. Parted like friends.

I got your letters 114, 116, 117 with the cuttings. They are all right; only newspapers are prohibited.

I was very interested in your description how it all got to the press. Our Maisky is not very bright if the English journalists could provoke him so easily. But sooner or later it had to get known. The letter of Rutherford is very good form; he puts the question widely. I recognise, feel, how he, my beloved old man, embosses his thoughts. The best thing for us is to be silent; abroad they will storm and will stop. I personally will get into a corner and shall be silent. To the devil with them all. Even without it, it is unpleasant enough to be disturbed.

8 May 1935
Moscow

I receive all your letters well, but did not write to you because I was busy writing a letter to comrade Molotov, with relation of the present polemics and of my impossibility to take part in them. This is not approved here, and I wrote an explanation in details why I behave like this, on 8 pages. I was very sincere, but will they value my sincerity I don't know? But to-day I am sending the letter. When all the sharpness of the moment will pass, I shall let you know its contents. I do not understand, why ours are so agitated; it is better not to take notice of it all. When they detained me, they had to realise that if they want me to work probably the others also could want it. But of course the mistake of ours is that up till now they approach me as a wrecker. They look after me well and count this as the main thing, and completely ignore my mentality.

Yesterday the institute received a very good car, big and comfortable, and which I can use as director and while I am director. It is rather fun to have such a car. When I came to the door of the Metropole the porter helped me out as if I was an old man. I even cursed.

Yesterday I also got the shares of the loan, so I have now shares. When I lived in capitalist England, never bought any shares or loans, and always drove the car (it is true my own), and here the loan and the car with driver. But all this is laughter through tears. Perhaps at last the letter I wrote will make them change their opinion about me.

Yesterday came Talmud. He is staying not far from me, and we drink coffee together in the morning. He is a nice fellow and urges me to come to Leningrad. You know it is amusing with Pavlov's illness. I wanted to potter a bit in Semenoff's institute and he got frightened. Says you better ask permission, etc. He cannot refuse me, but feels more quiet this way.

Yes, "O" yesterday again tried to intimidate me. They will be excited and then it will pass. . . .

I am waiting for the drawing of children. You are more kind now. You cannot imagine how I miss them sometimes.

Here the weather is warmer but the trees are not yet green, and you have probably the almond over. For the children it is probably quite nice to play in the garden.

Thank Andrew for the greeting and tell him to write me, my dear. Tell him daddy wants him to write a letter like Sereja. I shall be pleased.

Well to-day the letter is short, but my finger is sore from writing, so do not be cross.

P.S. Do not send cuttings. It will only make me worried, as it has probably all sorts of nonsense and I hate the press.

9 May 1935
Moscow

To-day unpleasant news—they give almost no tickets to the theatre. I don't know why, but apparently this is a punishment. Here I feel myself like a pupil. If I do something the tutor does not want me to do, they put me in a corner. And my tutor is Mezhlauk. But now that I got the wireless I don't mind.

Everyone is discussing the speech of Stalin.[28] It is really quite a remarkable one, and energetic.

I feel great apathy. If I talk with someone I have to lay down afterwards. But my mood is not bad. As if I live under an anaesthetic, nothing gives me pleasure, but nothing upsets me either. I think this is natural adaptation; by this means I am guarding my nervous system and making it automatically less impressionable. Perhaps this is why I don't even want to do science, as it always agitates me.

11 May 1935
Moscow

I have not much strength now, or to say it more correctly all goes into thinking.

To-day I wrote a letter to Mezhlauk commenting on Rutherford's, saying

---

28. Kapitza is possibly referring to one of several speeches made about this time in which Stalin called for a new "Soviet humanism." Hitherto, he said, stress had been laid almost entirely on the "Soviet machine," while the population endured suffering and privation. But now that the machine was strong, greater care must be taken of the rank and file of workers. Kapitza must have been wryly amused that the Soviet press developed a campaign that included better care of specialists. See *The Times*, 15 and 16 May, and 1 June 1935.

Valeri I. Mezhlauk and Vyacheslav Molotov. Courtesy of the Cambridge
University Library.

the main thing in it is the complaint of the representatives of the scientific
world that an important work is interrupted, and that the mentality of a scientist is not understood. And that the letter is a friendly advice and that it is
ridiculous for me to interfere.

I even feel my influence on Rutherford. How he is talking about the Soviet is very good and kind, but I am afraid here they did not appreciate it
enough.

I am sending to you the photo of Mezhlauk (left) and Molotov (right).[29]
Show it to Rutherford; he is a good judge of people's souls by their faces.
And ask him what he thinks in this case. Mezhlauk has a nice little face, and
even though I am cross with him occasionally, I like him quite a lot. But he
must diminish his airs. Well, I think it is just a bad habit, which is difficult to
get rid of. You know here in the Academy I was told that I do not make myself important enough. Someone asked me to come; well, I went. And then I
was told that I must not have done it, as this person must have gone to me!
Well I don't understand it yet. I am rather free and had no difficulty in
going.

29. See the photograph on this page.

I spend pleasant time in the Academy. Here all know about the English press, as it is read a lot. Do *not* send me cuttings.

I had your 120 letter and as usual was very pleased. It is a great comfort to me. Specially when they want to punish me. But the unfortunate part is it is difficult to punish me, if not quite impossible, as nothing can be worse than my position; no work, no you, no peace, no Rutherford, no comfort, what else can one do with me?

I interrupted the letter as Mezhlauk telephoned that Molotov will see me after to-morrow, and hopes all will finish well. This quite upset me. Well, we shall see what happens.

31 May 1935
Moscow

Well, you ask for the details. Listen how I see it all. I had a great moral change. It is not clear to me in the whole, but here are its main factors which you ought to know. You know that I always wanted to take part in the building of our science. I always said to you I could not imagine the socialist state without science in the leading part. And I even now believe in it and believe that the science in the Union will reach unknown heights. This is why I always wanted to take part in the organisation of this process, which will happen even without me, but to do my share I wanted. So as soon as I was transferred from the scene in Leningrad to Moscow, in January, I at once took part, or to be correct, expressed my wish to take part in the reconstruction of the Academy. And then all this time I took initiative in this direction, wrote reports, discussed questions with Mezhlauk, etc. Now it is exactly 6 months of these efforts and they ended in nothing. Whose fault is it? Perhaps mine. I did not know how to approach, or perhaps the time is not ripe. One can write a whole treatise on the subject, but one thing is clear, more efforts are useless. And I definitely decided that in the Union I will only take up science and I will definitely refuse all social work. To tell the truth, even, it is not necessary to refuse, as I was never approached. This is of course a serious decision, and if I took it, it only was after hard thinking. Perhaps you will think it is foolish, as I absolutely am on the side of our socialist reconstruction, without being a member of the Party, and of course in my own convictions I do not differ from them. And with our scarcity in such people between our scientists it might seem from the first quite a foolish decision. But this is not so, and notwithstanding it all I shall have to take the position of Pavlov. It means that of a man who sits in his den, follows everything and from there tries to make his voice heard, without taking any active part in life. This is more peaceful for me and more pleasant for others, and it simplifies the position. Only one question is left—my science. Well, so it is now. I am trying to recreate my Cambridge work here, but I have no trust that I shall succeed in this. I wrote about it to comrade Molotov: "I look at this venture as possible (in the present conditions) as to make a hole with a penknife in a stone wall." Monte Cristo did it, but it took half of his life to do it. But while I am Director of the Institute I must do a definite program which was given to me, and with the greatest effectiveness. But of course I write letters "upwards" pointing out all the difficulties, etc. I shall write about it in more details later on; this is very long and dull. Once, I had to resign because they wanted to make me do something which I counted as not possible for me. Later it was withdrawn, and the "status quo" was left. But I fear, or better I am certain, that in another 2-3 months I shall have to resign and to go away from it all. I cannot see any other issue. Of course, if all with the laboratory apparatus will come right then perhaps it will be possible to find another issue. But the instinctive feeling tells me that if ours will go on behaving like idiots, as they did it till now, then nothing will come out of it all. I am not listened to, and no one asks my advice. They only order, when I know so much better how one has to act.

Mezhlauk thinks that the buying of the laboratory is only a question of money. It is difficult to imagine a more foolish attitude. He said to me: "They will ask 200,000, well we shall offer 10,000 and will come to an agreement somewhere." I warned him from the beginning that he was mistaken. Maisky seems to be not much cleverer. Well it is their business. And so in 2-3 months I resign. All the press noise will stop by then, and ours will be more quiet. But the building which will be done will not be wasted, because in any case the country will get a first rate institute. I put in it all my English experience, which will be useful here. Only a long passage with special foundation will be useless, and a balcony, but all the other parts will be useful to any institute. The organisation, the position, the dwellings, all are done exemplary. I put in it enough energy, who will get will not curse me. Of course they will be cross with me for my resignation. And so in 2-3 months I shall be a free man, with only one difference that it will be of no further use to exploit me, and then I think they will let me in peace. In one year all will forget me, and in two completely. During this time, I shall quietly and little by little be born again. Will be born like a harmless physiologist. I shall not need the institute, no expensive machines, etc. I shall be 43, and I shall have enough energy, if my head will not give up, that I shall be able to conquer a position for myself. This is necessary for the scientist to be able to join in the circle of colleagues. This is the picture, or to be correct, the plan which I am following. Why not take physiology straightaway, as I did ½ a year ago? The explanation is simple. First, ours still see in it a bad meaning, a certain demonstration, and so are cross. And as I already made them sufficiently cross, and shall still make even more so, well I must not overdo it. I after all like them, however stupid or strange it seems. And secondly, my head is in such a state, that to concentrate on the quiet scientific thought I cannot. Even without physiology my head and nerves are so stretched that it will be good if they will not give up. I want to know your opinion. As for you, I think you will have to come and the children will have to stay another year in England. With all the uncertainty and the possibility of troubles, and also "punishment" for the "obstinacy," why should the children join in it. Well, if physiology will not come out, even because of the material questions, I will have to take up one of many other professions, as I know how to do many things. And I remember not one single work which I did in which I did not find something interesting and new.

Well, this is all about me. I think I wrote very clearly and fully about myself. As for my letter to Molotov, of course I cannot send it to you. But in any case, as always was I have no secrets, but this is not done and people might get upset. But the letter comes to the following: that at the moment I am here extremely unhappy. I say why in details, only tell about the moral conditions and the scientific conditions for my work, all that I lived through these 8 months. Then I say that this did not move my faith in the work, which was done by the Soviet under the leadership of the Communist Party, and that with all my thought and soul I am on their side,—"and should I have been a politician or economist I shall only be too proud to be in the ranks of the COM. P. But fate decided differently, and made me into a scientist, and as a scientist I must naturally try to find the conditions in which I can more fully exploit my scientific gifts. This wish is a natural one. Without my apparatus, books, comrades-scientists, and rudely interrupted in my scientific work in the most interesting place, I am absolutely unhappy, broken, sad and useless. If you would know how to treat a scientist you would have understood my condition without any effort. But having a deep faith in the internationalism of science, I believe that real science must be outside political passions and struggles, however much one would want to involve it in it. I believe that the scientific work which I did all my life is the property of the whole of humanity, whenever I was doing it." This was the end of my letter. I still stand on the point of view that we only had a misunderstanding and the main and basic thing is the mistrust which I cannot break down. I must put down my arms and the plan I wrote to you in this letter is nothing else but an honourable capitulation and a retreat on the new positions: "Physiology". . . .

To-morrow the doctors will examine me, and your father too for company. My head aches less. I shall write more often now.

5 June 1935
Boloshovo

I am already four days here and feel much better. You know how quickly I get better when I am in the country. . . . My heart is better too; I could row for almost one hour. It is clear all is the question of the nerves, and so the injections, etc. are nonsense.

I have a more quiet mood. I think it is because of the decision I reached. I wrote about it in the last letter—I mean only to do pure science in the Union and not to take any part in the social work. So let the science in the Union develop just as it wants to. Sooner or later it will go the right way, and all I could do was to make this "later" be a bit "sooner." There will be no tragedy in it and I will fight no more and will not try to make our people cleverer. This will only make me lose my head. Well, it means that in future I picture a very secluded work, purely scientific, and very possibly in physiology. All this is very silly because I never will be able to have the same conditions of work as in Cambridge, and if it was any sense to transfer my work here it was because I could influence the rise of science in the Union. But as now the question of my taking part in the life of the country is excepted, then all this is very stupid. But a rude violence is always stupid. A clever man can always find a way to force the other to do what he wants without apparent violence, so the other would want to do it too. To say it clearly, to change the way of violence into mutual agreement. But ours here count it as harmful for the prerogatives of the Government to come to agreement with a citizen. What an extraordinary stupidity. Of course, for any business it is better that the man who is doing it would think or even deceive himself that he is doing it by his own wish and not by order. The order is only needed for soldiers. What they are doing are clearly senseless deeds, which cannot be excused by any reasons. For a revolutionary army full of enthusiasms of course the orders have no more reason; there the discipline is needed to co-ordinate the movements of units. To the scientists all this is appliable a thousand times more. Up to the time when we shall create such moral conditions in which every scientist will make all possible to work in his country, and one need not be afraid that he will escape, till then it is difficult to count on the development and flourishing of the science. All this is elementary simple and easily done, but it is extraordinary difficult to explain and to make them understand it. "But one in the field is not a soldier." It seems that the time is not yet ready for all this, but for every man who even slightly understands these questions, all I say must sound as elementary truths. I must bend my head as the victim of the time, and the only thing is to retire in my den, as did Pavlov, and sit there and do my own things. This will be possible to arrange, not so well as in Cambridge, but well enough as not to count this time as lost in life. It seems something can be done, but I am worried by one question. This is you dear.

Well, see what may happen: I could work one, two, three years in physiology; at the end they will be bored to keep and torture me. For me all the world is open for work, and one only can keep me by force let us say for 5 years. People sat in prison, in lunatic asylums, were banished, for the same periods and in much worse conditions than mine. I have all the life conditions, the material ones all right; only the spiritual are bad. At the end they will have to give me back my freedom. The wives were waiting like the famous Penelope. So do wait till all will get clear, and be courageous and don't get upset, and obey your husband who is still clever.

Well now about F. E. Smith.[30] I understand his point of view very well. The best [Englishman to visit me] is F. E. Smith or Hardy, or Jeans, Hopkins, that sort of man. Winstanley, Simpson, Dirac, etc., all are suitable.[31] One must not put it off for long; I am certain ours will have nothing against this visit.

Then I do not want to see the physiologists and all the congress,[32] and I would prefer to go away for the time. I want to know your opinion about this.

Will you please send me the most important of the press articles, specially

30. Sir Frank Smith, Secretary of the Department of Scientific and Industrial Research, and Secretary of the Royal Society.

31. The visit was to ascertain how best to help Kapitza resume work in Russia, and specifically to see whether he was mentally and emotionally stable, after these agonizing months, to be able to benefit from such help. The men mentioned knew Kapitza well, most of them being Fellows of Trinity College. G. H. Hardy was a noted mathematician, James Jeans a theoretical physicist and astronomer, F. Gowland Hopkins a Nobel laureate for his work in biochemistry and then president of the Royal Society, Denys A. Winstanley and Rev. F. A. Simpson were historians, and P. A. M. Dirac was a Nobel Prize-winning theoretical physicist.

32. The International Congress of Physiology met in Moscow during the summer of 1935. Foreign delegates were extremely well treated, for this was the first international meeting held in the Soviet Union since the Revolution and the government wished to signify clearly its new desire and policy for scientific contacts abroad. But this desire did not extend to sending young Russians to foreign laboratories; furthermore, the government apparently was not interested in exchanging journals. Both points were noted by A. V. Hill, an eminent British physiologist who was well aware of Kapitza's history ("The Fifteenth International Congress of Physiology," *Science*, 82 [13 Sept. 1935], 240–41, and "Foreign journals in the USSR," *Science*, 82 [6 Dec. 1935], 550). Also the hospitality extended to visitors did not last long. *The Times* of

of the foreign press. Give a description and your opinion about it. If you did not read, then ask Rutherford or someone else. I may be asked to discuss this question, so I must not be in the dark. They accuse me and I don't even know. And so straight away give me this information. I thought of not taking any interest in it, but now it is difficult to avoid it.

Well, dear do not worry. I understand all very well and see it perhaps very much better than you think. I know people pretty well.

7 June 1935
Moscow

I am very glad you are sending my things with the physiologists. The custom officials could not say anything as they will be distributed between 10-15 people. How foolish and stupid that my own things I must get with such tricks. One of the many proofs of the idiocy of our people. This taking duty on my own things, after I was promised the full assistance—well how can one trust them? How can one trust them in big things, when in the details they cannot keep their promise? But we shall be more clever with you my dear, and I think if you will be very energetic, you will send me a supply of things for another year.

I would like very much to have a camera; there is probably something new out. Send me the catalogues from Turners. . . . Well, all these are just toys, nonsense. But I am so unspoiled now that I could do with toys. You know here they do not spoil me, far from it, and I forgot the delicacy in the attitude towards me. It seems to me, here there exist a "valuta" attitude and "non valuta." Well, with me it is the non valuta. But my hide is pretty strong and I could hold my own for another 5 years of the same treatment.

To-day I finished my affairs in the town and am going back this evening to the sanatorium. I will do the same for several weeks. However much our idiots would like to ruin my health, I will find a way of keeping my nerves in order. Do not worry about me.

Well, if at last our idiots will get more reasonable and will let me out of the harem (I am like a white slave), I don't see why all this fuss could not end for the satisfaction of all. Of course ours are whimpering something about

---

22 Oct. 1937 described the spy mania affecting Russia, specifically a pamphlet issued by the head of the State Security Police in the Leningrad area saying that foreigners, especially members of scientific delegations, often are agents of foreign secret services. At the 1935 International Congress of Physiology, it charged, several professional spies posed as scientists.

prestige, but this is all nonsense. They are not such complete idiots as in Western Europe, so as not to see because of the prestige what is useful. It seems to me that one day they will see Dostoevsky called his most genius hero "Idiot."

Well, once more I ask you to send me all that was in the newspapers. Your [views], and *systematically*, send it, so I should know what is happening. At first I thought not to take any interest in it but now I see that without it, it would be rather difficult. Ours think of it more than I think it is necessary. One thing strikes me: my impression is such that they thought such attitude in the press is impossible, and even now all the delicacy of the tone of Rutherford they do not value enough. They do not know how Rutherford can curse. . . . Well, no one knows he is an old farmer and little by little he is aroused, always keeping in reserves some untouched, yet, curses. I know him well. Of course you can do little. He is like me and never listens to anybody but himself.

Why Webster is not coming?[33] But the best thing will be if Cockcroft must come, that he should come with others, Hopkins, or Keynes, Laski or others in the same style.[34] But all must be arranged strictly officially through Maisky. Otherwise I shall not talk to them. . . . Try again to send the New Statesman and Manchester Guardian. Perhaps they are again allowed; devil only knows. What is Leipunsky doing?

19 June 1935
Leningrad

Arriving in Leningrad I received your letters 139, 140. But I have not got your letters 134, 137, 138, and also the press cuttings. I was very pleased with all these letters and shall hurry to answer all your questions.

First, Webster is a very good choice. I also think that he must come as soon as possible, and must have with him all the materials of the conversations between Maisky and Rutherford, as all this they do not tell me. I am sympathetic with all my heart to all that will bring a peaceful solution, but I have not a slightest idea of what and where is being done. This is why up till now I did not take up any kind of diplomatic attitude, but said all exactly as I

33. William Webster, a postdoctoral research worker in the Mond Laboratory, who contemplated a trip earlier in the year, was again considering going to Moscow.

34. John Cockcroft, who ran the Mond Laboratory after Kapitza's departure, later shared the Nobel Prize in physics with E. T. S. Walton for their nuclear transformation experiments using accelerated particles. John Maynard Keynes was the noted economist.

felt it. This is the only policy possible in my position. I want peace and good to the Union, and especially to science. It is a pity, but have they lost faith in our scientists, or is it just a habit, ours here, to trust me in absolutely nothing?

The same is about the talks with foreigners, which Laski wants. What can I say to these gentlemen? The truth! Nothing else. But would ours here like it? But I am ready to talk to them if you and Rutherford think it necessary, but in the following conditions. First and absolutely necessary that during the whole of the conversations Litvinoff would be present. Secondly that all the questions should be presented to me before the meeting and in the written form, and third that both of Laski's friends should be present at once. Fourth the conversation must take place after the visit of Webster; this is not essential, but desirable.

You must realise that I am completely in the dark, and understand nothing of what had happened. But so as not to get submerged, it is the best thing for me to sit in the dark and be silent. But I do not want that there should be any things spread about me which are definitely untrue and are harmful to the Union.

Of course ours behaved stupidly and meanly to me, but one must not accuse them in more than they are worth, and of course it is never too late yet to put it right.

Now about Rutherford's doubts. He must not be afraid for me. Tell him that it is a long time ago that I already got all that was best in life. And I am now like a dead volcano, or better a volcano which is temporarily dead (that's for you, so you will not worry). And who is better than my wife! I never met anyone in the world, and so you can completely rely on me, as I trust that you are a faithful and good wife. And all together if there were no you and no children, there would be no me now. All the present position would be easily and simply liquidated.

But perhaps if Rutherford writes to Maisky, and Maisky will promise him that you will have the facility of coming here for 3-4 weeks to arrange things. But if all can be peacefully ended this would be very nice.

Tell me, by the way, did Rutherford write again to The Times? What did make him write? I understand nothing. When will ours get a little more reasonable? What a mess is at the moment. Who wants what? But I suffer for all this.

Do let me know if you got my long letter of 16 pages; it ought to be interesting for you. If Webster will come ask him to bring my things, the ones I asked for. I am suffering without trousers; mine wore out. Everything began suddenly, catastrophically, to wear out, and here they don't know how to make them well.

When you will get this letter, wire when approximately will Webster come, just like this, William coming about such and such date.

Better sooner and better in Moscow there will be more opportunity to talk to people.

24 July 1935
Moscow

Yesterday I received your letter 155 and I am very happy. As about the lectures about the industry, this is all sheer nonsense and lies. First of all, I never promise anything, even if I know I could possibly do it. And then, too many tales are attached to my name, and to take notice of them it is only to make oneself worried. I am not interested in gossip or tales. And of course Rutherford is clever enough to do the same. I think he makes fun of you when he tells you such things. He knows me well enough. And I fear that you do not understand and do not value enough why it is so important for me to get away from the scene and as you say to dry off. At the end one gets tired to listen to all these talks, and only going into such completely innocent domain as physiology, I could end all the silly talk and start pure scientific work, so that no one would touch me.

In all this time I did not draw nor build one single project of apparatus, and except for reading books and articles about physiology I did not do any scientific or technical work. I neither gave lectures nor published any scientific work. And definitely stated to all in the Union that only would do purely scientific work and nothing else. Except consultations, but they never were asked for. And so I think all must be quite clear for you after all I said.

It is my rule, I never lie and never talk idly. I am afraid Rutherford got entangled in some diplomacy. This does happen to him occasionally, but otherwise he is a straightforward and honest man.

I have not yet seen Mezhlauk. As soon as I shall see him I shall write to you. I shall accept with pleasure the decision which will satisfy everybody, but for this they must basically change their attitude to me. If this will not be done, then I see no other way out but the one which I wrote to you, to go away from the scene as far as it is possible. This is not my fault. I am sincerely fond of our idiots, and they do wonderful things and it will all make history. And I was prepared to do all to help them, and even now I shall do all what is in my power to help them. But what can be done if they understand nothing in science, or more correctly they do not know how to create science. But for this it is clear one has to wait till they will get wiser. And to take up the policy of Semenoff or Joffé, to compromise and to wriggle, this I don't know and don't want to do. They (the idiots), of course, can get clever tomorrow, and perhaps in 5-10 years. That they will get clever, there is no doubt about it. The life will make them do it. But the question is—when. I tried to hasten it, but up till now without results. But you can be certain that from the first day till now I never compromised with my conscience, and I am certain I shall never do it. I say all the time what I think, even if I am alone. No pleasures of life will seduce me. Nothing will intimidate me and nothing will seduce me. I feel myself very strong, my conscience is quite clear. I have not one single action for which I could be ashamed in front of our people, country, government and even communist party. On the contrary, I think I did a lot for them and for the Soviet science, even though they don't want to acknowledge it. I do not want thanks, but my internal feeling, that I can hold high my head, gives me happiness. This feeling gives me the minimum of happiness possible without you, children and work, but necessary to keep the wish to live.

25 July 1935
Moscow

Yesterday I wrote you a letter where I told you that all about the lecture is a lie, and that all that I am doing here is to take part of pure science, which has rather a bad time. And I don't do anything else except physiology, and will not be able to until I shall have the people and assistants from my laboratory.

Yesterday I went near Zvenigorod to Semenoff's. There is also Frumkin[35] and his wife. But what I like is to meet Bach. We are definitely friends with the old man. He often tells me that there are not many people with whom he likes to talk as much as with me. It is true we do agree with him in many things; he, very quietly, keeps up his ideas. Of course I also do it, but not quietly. Perhaps the difference of the temperament or the age plays its part; he is 35 years older than I am, almost twice. We went together to Moscow.

It is remarkable how he, A. K. Semenoff, cannot make people round him do what he wants. He is wonderfully clever himself, exceptionally clever, and this is his only power. But as soon as he is pressed, he shrinks. On discussing how to bring to life an idea, Semenoff drew on the table such line ⌁➤. We, with Bach, think that a straight line is the shortest distance between two points.

---

35. Alexander Frumkin, a physical chemist.

They spend three hours talking with comrade B.[36] You do not know him; he is a very important party member. He is put at the head, to direct, or to organise, the scientific and research work in the Union. This is for the first time that in the Union, a really important comrade is at the head of the organisation to look after the scientific life. This is very good and it must be acknowledged. One says that comrade B. spent in Joffé's institute seven hours. It seems that he seriously has taken up his work. At the moment he just curses everyone, gently. I think he probably thinks like a certain general, that there is no harm in cursing, and might be some good even. But of course for a man who never had anything to do with scientists before it is difficult to grasp at once all the situation of our abandoned "scientific economy." Semenoff, Frumkin, and Bach were rather disappointed with the visit, but why I could not elucidate. Comrade B. at the beginning has taken a very definite side for practical science, but at the end he was not so firm. I think perhaps it was only because he wanted to make our academicians take up the side of pure science, and so to show themselves. This is quite right and clear; how can he find out about our scientists and their wishes otherwise? But it was a lively talk. For instance, Semenoff: "And so you think that no theory is necessary?" B. "Do you take me for an idiot, or what?", etc. I decided to get away from all the social side of our science and only do scientific work, so I don't think I shall meet B., but it is interesting to follow it all. I would like to see Joffé. One says he is very pleased with his talk with B., and from the other side B. points him out as how not to direct a scientific institute. There, just find the truth. But some of the remarks of B. I liked. He points out that one must not boast with the number of scientific publications or the number of scientific workers. He did notice an amateur way in the work of Joffé. This is also true. But I am interested, did B. find it all by himself or does he have a prompter?

But there is certain light on our scientific front. It is noticed. Of course one shall make mistakes, as usual, but they will reach a right solution sooner or later. And sooner they will take up this question, sooner they will find a solution. But as in France after the revolution, there was a great swing in the science, and so it will be here.

26 July 1935
Boloshovo

I came here yesterday and shall stay till to-morrow. Dirac is coming on the 28th; there is a wire from him from Irkutsk. Yesterday I had a talk with "O."

36. Karl Ianovich Bauman, who in 1934 became chief of the party Central Committee's Department of Science and Scientific and Technological Discoveries and In-

He does complain all the time that I don't love him, and that he is so kind to me but I am not fair to him, etc. My position is difficult; I cannot disagree with it, but at the same time I don't want to make our relations even worse. In normal conditions I should just put him in his place, saying, just do your business, and do not touch these questions, but at the moment it was impossible. If, as it seems, I shall have to resign, he will be able to finish the job and adapt the institute for some work. My leaving will not touch anyone; at the moment there is no scientific work. In these three months I not only did not read, but did not sign one single paper. So I wrote to comrade Molotov that I am as much a director as Shah of Persia. So I can leave it all at the moment. Ours cannot even curse, because I warned them several times that without people and apparatus it is not worth while to build the institute. (There are 4 letters on this subject, one to the government, one to Mezhlauk, one to Molotov, and also a statement to the Academy of Sciences Presidium). Mezhlauk does not know when he will see me, but there is no hurry. Even better, let them get used to the idea of my resignation; it will pass easier.

I never wrote to you in all details the story about the parcel, I think one of the most scandalous of all. When I just before the new year decided to agree with a lot, so as to rebuild my scientific work here, I was promised to be put in such conditions that I shall have not to worry about everyday details, like clothes, and all shall be done to make me as comfortable as in Cambridge. Well of course I did not count on this, but even if half would be done it would be good. But the main thing for me, it was important to state the wish to put me in good conditions, and the sincere and good attitude to me. So as to check it, I asked for a fur hat and a suit. I was detained without warning. We came by car with the minimum of clothes, and I feel the need in it even up to now. Well "O" promised that he will arrange all, but did nothing. In the shop at which I could shop there was nothing I needed. Well, the hat I bought for valuta in the Torgsin. Without it I would catch a cold and my head is, so to say, the reason for all this hullabaloo. And the suit I ordered in Insnab (it is already seven months that I cannot get it, but to the devil with it, it is so badly done). Well as you see, no care. After I told "O" what about you sending all I was needing, he said of course, "I shall arrange all for you without duty. I think you have right to it." Well, your famous parcel arrives, the duty on it is 3500 rubles, a big sum even for here. "O" goes to the customs, but can do nothing. He asks me to write a demand to Mezhlauk. I am already cross: to ask for what was already promised to me.

---

ventions. For biographical information, see the *Great Soviet Encyclopedia* (New York: Macmillan; London: Collier Macmillan, 1973), vol. 3, pp. 80–81.

Perhaps I did write a naughty letter, but it translated very accurately my thoughts. As result, I got an answer that my request is against the law and cannot be granted. And so I paid for the parcel; otherwise I still should be sitting without shoes or shirts. But it is still unknown to me why, if my things should have been sent by rail, they are free of duty, and if by post they are not. In these points of jurisprudence it is difficult to understand anything. But from that moment I felt myself offended and tricked. I cannot know all the endless parts of our law, but even if I knew it, it would not have helped me. There is none, and there was none, good and kind attitude to me. And how without it can I start a great work in the country?

This episode of the parcel has shown all the abnormality of my position here and, after it, all went badly, though I doubt that one can blame me for anything at all. I have done all I was asked for (of course I could not lie, by order), did not refuse anything, and I am absolutely obedient. What else do they want? I cannot understand.

The weather is very bad, rain, rain and rain, All the summer is like this. They say it is not always like this. I was offered to go to the South, but I don't want it. All must be cleared at last. All this nonsense is dragging on for a whole year. Perhaps it is my fault. Better was not to meet them at anything, but be stubborn as a donkey. But I wanted to do good. But now I think I shall liquidate it all. I shall try to do it as peacefully as possible, without fuss or cursing. I will restrain myself.

28 July 1935
Moscow

A day before yesterday came "O" and said Mezhlauk could see me yesterday. Well yesterday I went to see him and this is the result of our talks. I don't yet know if one can call it positive, but one cannot call it negative. On the surface Mezhlauk was very unpleasant, but this I expected. But he did not say no to the questions in my letter to Molotov, so there is no direct motive for my resignation. He wanted me to ring up Rutherford on the telephone. I pointed out my plan of peace and termination of the conflict; if it will be accepted, I think all can be normal.[37] My offer was not blankly refused by Mezhlauk and if the comrades of Mezhlauk will agree to it, then it will be accepted. So I wrote my plan down on paper, and sent it already yesterday to Mezhlauk, and shall wait for a reply. Now a lot depends from

37. Aside from trust in him and obtaining the contents of the Mond Laboratory, there are no indications what this plan comprised.

Rutherford, and the best way of conversations would be through Webster, and it seems that his coming could be arranged.

But what really touched me, and gave me pleasure, is our conversation about you. I pointed out that all the conflict without you would have taken quite a different aspect, but only because of you, there was no outburst of anti-Soviet character. Mezhlauk says that he often heard about you as a very clever woman (blush), and they all think that you must come as soon as possible and be my help. That no pressure will be brought up against you, that they promise you complete freedom of going and coming between England and here, as much as you like it, and that only when you would like it here you could come here with children. For this sentence I gave Mezhlauk full mark, fine fellow, many sins were pardoned him for it. This is how one must treat not only you but everybody. Then Mezhlauk said that you will be given a passage on the boat, that I must not worry and that Maisky will let you know about it, and that nothing can happen as there is no better thing than his and Molotov's word, and nothing else is wanted. I think if my plan will be accepted, then I see nothing against your coming for a month or month and half. When you will get this letter, begin quietly to arrange things for the journey. Ask for a return visa to England, arrange family affairs, and let Granny do the housekeeping. It seems that you will have to go backwards and forwards. I am very pleased with it all; there is some possibility of peaceful solution to the whole conflict. Now I am expecting to hear again from them. But if now ours will let the opportunity pass, then I do not know if it would be possible to find another opportunity for a peaceful solution. It is possible I shall ring you up on the telephone. I was told that ours have nothing against my conversations with the physiologists. I am rather afraid that with you will happen the same thing as with the parcel. It is always uncertain once you are cheated, not to feel you will be done in again. Well, we shall see. But I do want to see you.

⋘ 5 ⋙

To Start Anew

Whatever the cause for Rutherford's optimism in early May 1935, Kapitza's permanent detention seemed certain by the end of that month. Whether it was the intransigence of the Soviet government or the resignation to his predicament exhibited in Kapitza's letters to his wife, the question changed from how to extract Kapitza from his captivity to how best to help him resume scientific work in Russia.

Possibly, one of the documents that helped to crystallize this change of attitudes in Cambridge was a letter from Kapitza to Rutherford. As long as he had hopes of being released, Kapitza had refrained from writing, believing it would weaken his moral case. This rare communication, reproduced below, therefore heralded his recognition of the futility of further efforts, and its tone would not have been lost on Rutherford. Even more, Kapitza's letter to Molotov at the same time, a copy of which was sent to Rutherford, and which also is printed here, spells out clearly Kapitza's willingness to pursue science in Russia.

[mid-May 1935]
Moscow

My dear Professor,
   I was informed that the case of my retention got into the papers. Whatever is the point and the object of this discussion, I only would love to keep myself completely out of it. But as a point of fairness I would only like that everyone concerned should know that first of all, I am and always was in sympathy with the work of the Soviet Government on the reconstruction of Russia, on the principle of socialism, and I am prepared to do scientific work here. Secondly the Soviet Government does its best to build me a laboratory.

There are indeed points about which we disagree, specially regards the treatment of the question of the pure science, as they are far greater valuing of the solutions of applied problems, and also we disagree about the most efficient way of dealing with scientists, but no doubt there is the best intention to develop science in the Union.

Personally I am very miserable indeed that all this happened. I miss you, my laboratory and specially my work and it is not to be expected that I soon will be able to resume it, and all this makes me very unhappy.

The stupidity of the created position is that it is based on complete misunderstanding as everyone concerned really acts with the best intentions.

My most kind regards and my love.

Yours ever,
Peter Kapitza

P.S. I have no objections for you to make part or in all this letter public.

[mid-May 1935]
Moscow

Comrade Molotov,

Here is the letter to Rutherford and its translation. Tell me what you wish to change in it. My opinion is that it honestly portrays the present position and my "credo." I am not writing about the buying of the laboratory until there will be a definite answer, and then of course I shall need to know all the details of the conversation. I want to tell you once more that Rutherford is quite the most remarkable and unique man and that I respect and love him very much and will never do anything that can hurt him or be unpleasant to him.

As to my wife's visit is it possible for comrade Maisky to let her know that it would be quite safe for her to come for a fortnight to the Union to arrange for the moving of the children? You must not be offended about this but you know yourself that your ways with people make them nervous sometimes. If I am now and again threatened, I do not mind it, I am only sad, but I do not get frightened. But there is no need for my wife to live through it all. I do want so much that all should finish well, and at the moment all is very bad. It is not clear to me what you do value in me? and what you need me for? You only learned recently about me and managed very well without me before. You thought that I was useful to English science and so could be useful to you. Is this not a mistake? English people drink Epsom salt but the Russians do very well without it. You said to me that you got plenty of Kapitzas among your youth. I am certain that you have got not only Kapitzas but even super Kapitzas, but with your methods you will never "fish" them out of the 160,000,000. At the moment you must ask for help from England through Rutherford.

I never will admit that the attitude shown to me is the right one. I am not offended for myself, I am afraid for the other Kapitzas. This I see very clearly and cannot pass it in silence for the sake of the Union.

It would be such a good thing if you would trust me at last and give me my freedom. I should be happy and work again. You would not be cross with me and lose time. And when the laboratory is built, I shall start work on the Vorobievy Gory [Sparrow Hills] for the glory of the USSR and for the use of all the people.

Peter Kapitza

Rutherford's task now was to establish contact with Kapitza in order to see best how to help him resume his scientific work. Direct communication by mail finally was feasible, now that Kapitza was willing to write to others besides his wife. But more than this, Rutherford needed to know Kapitza's mental state—whether he was still capable of benefiting from material aid—and this required sending to Russia someone who knew him. Fortunately, Edgar Adrian, Fellow of Trinity College, like Kapitza a Royal Society Research Professor, and 1932 Nobel laureate in physiology, planned to attend the Physiology Congress in Moscow and accepted Rutherford's commission. Because there had been some previous ambiguity regarding whether anyone would be permitted to see Kapitza, Adrian carried with him Ambassador Maisky's latest letter to Rutherford assuring him that foreigners were free to speak to all Russian citizens.[1]

Once in Moscow, in August 1935, Adrian had no difficulty in seeing Kapitza. Likewise P. A. M. Dirac, the mathematical physicist who held the chair once occupied by Cambridge's most famous "old boy," Isaac Newton, and who paid an extended visit to Russia that summer. Dirac, who received the Nobel Prize in 1933 and who was a foreign member of the Soviet Academy of Sciences, was also a long-time member of the "Kapitza Club." Like Adrian, therefore, he was well qualified to assess Kapitza's situation and report it back to Rutherford.

1. Rutherford letter to E. D. Adrian, 31 July 1935.

They found Kapitza depressed, but calm and determined about his future; given something congenial, he was quite able to work. But the amount of help he wanted was staggering: the contents of the Mond Laboratory, his two assistants, and retention of his Royal Society professorship or an equivalent title from Cambridge University. If this was impossible to arrange, he planned to leave physics altogether and begin a new career in physiology, hoping that in a few years Pavlov's training would enable him to lead a productive life and regain a measure of personal freedom. Under no circumstances could he foresee reestablishing his physics laboratory in Russia without major aid from England. As for the now-past possibility of obtaining his release through the international protests of scientists, Kapitza expressed his feeling that the strained relations between the outside world and the USSR that would have ensued made that course unjustifiable.[2]

So it was either physics or physiology. And if it was to be the former, Kapitza spelled out his requirements. His moral obligation to English scientists would be mitigated if the Soviet government transmitted to Britain a sum equal to the amount spent on him and his work during fourteen years, estimated at between £30,000 and £50,000. With Rutherford's agreement, he hoped that this money would be divided between the Royal Society and Cambridge University, with not less than 12 percent offered to Trinity College. Part of these funds would be used to defray the costs involved in arranging for shipment of the equipment from the Mond Laboratory, or to purchase duplicates of those items to remain in Cambridge. With a few specified exceptions, Kapitza asked for all the machines, measuring instruments, workshop tools, hardware supplies, and papers in the building, and even the clocks, wall fittings, and switchboards. He was considered greedy by some, who felt the Mond would be left nothing but a shell, but in fact Kapitza was now in a hurry to resume his work and quite realistic about the lack of supplies and equipment in Russia.

This realism extended to his need for skilled help in creating a

2. Kapitza's statement of 19 Aug. 1935, recorded by E. D. Adrian. Also E. D. Adrian letter to Rutherford, 21 Aug. 1935.

working laboratory. His government might construct a suitable building according to his plans,[3] but without talented and trained mechanics, who knew their way around large magnets and low temperature apparatus, Kapitza could not alone construct, erect, test, and use the equipment, or quickly train others to do so. Hence his request that Emil Laurmann, his research assistant, and Henry Pearson, the master mechanic in the Mond, spend three or four years with him, during which time Cambridge University would guarantee their present jobs and pension rights. His final point, that he retain a professorship in Great Britain, was meant to keep a toe in the door. Kapitza hoped that the Kremlin authorities eventually would allow him once again to travel abroad, and this time might come sooner if he had a position in which he was supposed to give a course of lectures each year. An annual visit to England, further, would be a good guarantee that he would have full control of his apparatus, for he would be able to report on his work.

Rutherford's reply, to be hand-carried by Anna Kapitza on her first visit with Peter after their year-long separation, was composed in the late summer of 1935. The Mond Laboratory, he said, was operating at a quiet pace, under his and Cockcroft's direction, until some new people gained experience. Then they planned an active program in the area for which the laboratory had been constructed, namely, cryogenics. Since the use of high magnetic fields was Kapitza's specialty, he intended to refrain from having this field pursued in Cambridge, unless there was no likelihood of Kapitza resuming this work in Moscow. Laurmann and Pearson were at present needed to train others and keep the laboratory running, but once they were no longer indispensable Rutherford would not stand in their way if they wished to join Kapitza temporarily. The matter of a professorship he dismissed in a few words: neither the university nor the Royal Society would consider such a proposal. As for Kapitza's desire to reimburse Cambridge University, Trinity College, and the Royal Society, Rutherford pointed out that their support was given freely and with-

3. Construction of the institute began in May 1935, with completion expected in about half a year (P. Rabinovitch letter to Rutherford, 3 Oct. 1935). Three and a half million rubles was provided for the task (*The Observer*, 28 Apr. 1935), and the laboratory would be about six times larger than the Mond (H. E. Pearson letter to J. D. Cockcroft, 8 July 1936).

out conditions, and no one expected compensation. The Soviet Embassy earlier had offered to purchase Kapitza's apparatus and, when Rutherford declined, Cahan then suggested it be donated.[4] This brash proposal too was declined, but Rutherford then, and now to Kapitza, indicated that he would be willing to send some of the equipment in the Mond, and duplicates of other pieces, to Moscow at Soviet expense, if Kapitza could not return to Cambridge.[5] The initiative now rested with the Soviet government to indicate specifically which items of apparatus they wanted and the price they were willing to pay.

Anna Kapitza left for Moscow at the end of September. Her departure had long been delayed by her unsuccessful efforts to obtain a promise, in writing or verbally in front of a witness, that she would be allowed out of Russia. She and G. I. Taylor, an eminent physicist and Fellow of Trinity College, in fact, had been ejected from the Soviet Embassy by Cahan, who showered them with abuse for requesting the assurance.[6] Her hope had been to visit with Peter for a month and to plan the eventual move of their children and belongings. Now, despite the fear of being detained, she determined from Dirac's reports that Peter needed her and that she would go. Yet, much to her surprise, when her passport was returned from the embassy in London it was stamped for travel in both directions.[7] Before her departure she confided to Rutherford that the Soviets had tried to compromise him in Kapitza's eyes, telling untrue stories in an effort to break his faith in Rutherford. It was not love of her or the children that kept Kapitza from suicide this past year, she said, but love of Rutherford and gratitude for all he had done.[8]

The formal steps to get Kapitza his apparatus now began. In early October 1935 a Russian official named Philip Rabinovitch presented Rutherford with his government's offer of £30,000 for the large generator and associated magnetic equipment, for duplicates of the hydrogen and helium liquefaction plants, and for other items in

---

4. S. B. Cahan letter to Rutherford, 16 Apr. 1935.

5. Rutherford letters to Kapitza, 28 Aug. and 25 Sept. 1935.

6. Anna Kapitza letter to Rutherford, 1 Sept. 1935, and G. I. Taylor letter to Rutherford, 31 Aug. 1935.

7. Anna Kapitza letter to Rutherford, 27 Sept. 1935.

8. Anna Kapitza letter to Rutherford, 25 Sept. 1935.

the laboratory. The Managing Committee of the Royal Society Mond Laboratory reported affirmatively to the Council of the Senate, which in turn reported its agreement to the whole of the university senate. With the concurrence of the Royal Society and the DSIR, the university thus was able to negotiate acceptance of these funds, which were used to replace the generator with a large electromagnet, useful for planned research at both low and normal temperatures, pay the DSIR for the apparatus to which it held title, purchase duplicates to be sent to Russia, repay the Royal Society for Kapitza's salary, which had been paid while he was in Russia, and establish a fund for future expenses of the Mond Laboratory.[9] Some believed that Rutherford had scored a diplomatic triumph in obtaining a settlement of £30,000, which was a large sum among those who knew what amounts normally went to support science. But, considering the expense of much of this "engineering" equipment, the continual requests from Kapitza for more and more items, and the time spent by Cockcroft and others in attending to the details, the figure does not seem excessively high. In fact, there were others who felt that Cambridge should have held out for £100,000.

The details of the ensuing shipment of materials are not pertinent to this story. Within the course of a year and with his customary good humor, Cockcroft did an enormous job in attending to the ever-increasing demands from an impatient Kapitza. For his part, Kapitza was plagued with his inability to obtain in Russia even the standard or off-the-shelf items so readily available in Britain. Thus, in addition to requests for scientific equipment, he urged Cockcroft to send such things as wall clocks, extension telephones, and door locks. And, he warned, be careful not to wrap anything in newspapers, for the Russian customs officials were furious when they had to remove such padding from an entire crate of hardware.

Kapitza suffered from periodic depressions, when he lost confidence in his abilities and his will to carry his needs through the bureaucracy. The question of freedom and trust still bothered him deeply and, try as he might, he could not make his countrymen understand that moral conditions for some are more important than

9. These two reports are dated 11 Oct. 1935 and 4 Nov. 1935, respectively.

material conditions.[10] Rutherford, one of the least introspective of men, repeatedly urged Kapitza to immerse himself in work and forget about the attitudes of others. Kapitza's troubles, he felt, would largely fall from him once his nose was kept close to the grindstone. Rutherford, further, told him frankly that he was complaining too much about the slow transferral of his equipment from Cambridge to Moscow. The university had stipulated that this effort must not seriously interfere with the normal research being pursued in the Mond Laboratory, and they were doing the best they could.[11] Kapitza's impish reply is printed below, as much for its insights about science and industry in Russia as for his own circumstances.

2 March 1936

My dear Professor,
    Your last letter I liked very much. Indeed you were not too kind in it, but I felt you so well, and it reminded me of all the innumerable cases when you called me a nuisance, etc. . . .
    I feel myself very miserable here; better than last year, indeed, but not so happy as I was in Cambridge. Anna's return brought me much comfort and happiness. In any way my family life is resumed and this is very important as I was here very lonely, quite alone, so the family is very much to me. Your letter reminded me of my happy years in Cambridge and then I felt you as you are, rough in the words and manners and good in your heart such as I like you, and this makes me feel rather happier. The lost Paradise!
    Some of my friends here call me Pickwick. I take the people better than they are and they think of me worse than I am. Probably this is right and this was the source of my misfortune. Nobody here appreciated that I tried to be useful and good to my country. They only saw in it all sorts of rotten things, and probably see some even now. How can I help? But the relation with authorities improved slightly, recently. I do not know what they have at the back of their minds, but at any case they seem to do everything possible to help me to resume my work. And in official relations you could not reasonably expect any more. The relations are official and formal.
    But my colleagues, the scientists, are very scared of me and behave like pigs. Do you see my Institute is attached to the Academy of Sciences, of

10. Anna Kapitza letter to Rutherford, 10 Nov. 1935.
11. Rutherford letters to Kapitza, 21 Nov. 1935 and 27 Jan. 1936.

which I am not a member,[12] but they govern my Institute. Fortunately I do
not need to assist their meetings and functions, but they have the say in the
running of the Institute. I cannot appoint a research student without their
sanctions, all my finances must be approved by the Council, etc. This would
not be bad, in general someone must look after the science, but what a
Council in this wonderful institution! The president is Karpinsky, he is 90!
In his young days he was not a bad geologist, nothing extraordinary, but
now he keeps going only by continous sleep. During the meeting of the
Council he sleeps with a happy and kind smile on his rather attractive face,
probably dreaming of his young days. He is a kind harmless man, an excellent president, never in anyone's ways.

[The following paragraph comes from a letter written four months later,
on 18 July 1936] The old Karpinsky, president of the Academy died. He
was 90, but still in working order. A kind soul and they say a good geologist, done a lot for the study of the earth crust. But indeed at 90 the man is a
slow working engine and it is not a surprise when it stops. He had an excellent state funeral, Stalin and Molotov carrying the urn to the Kremlin wall
where it was entombed. And then a huge public meeting in the Red Square.
This was to show the care of the government for the science. On the whole I
approve of such demonstrations, but in particular I think it is much better to
give attention to the living people. But this indeed is risky, when the man is
still alive he can always do a wrong thing one day, and about the dead man it
is certain that he will do no more wrong.

[The letter of 2 March resumes here] The two vice presidents are young
people for the Academy, as they are only 65. The first one Komaroff[13] is a
botanist. He knows what a plant is, and could tell a daisy from a poppy, and
probably he knows more names of plants than any other man in Russia, and
for this got into the Academy. . . . The second vice president is better, his
name also starts with a K, but is such a complicated one that I dare not to
spell it in English.[14] He is an electrical engineer, and was responsible for the
scheme of the electrification of the Union, a great achievement as I understand. But the man has got no scientific experience at all, he is a great
dreamer and very romantic. He has terrific schemes, but is lost in the details
and every day things. He is like the president a very kind man and he is very
popular in the Academy. He promises, while you speak to him a lot of
things, but never does a single one. Maybe this is better than to promise
nothing and to do nothing. But an inexperienced man like myself has for

12. Kapitza benefited from the great enlargement of the academy in 1929, being
elected a Corresponding Member that year. He became a full academician in 1939.
13. V. L. Komaroff, who succeeded A. P. Karpinsky as president, 1936–45.
14. G. M. Krjajanovsky.

few days some pleasant hopes, and this I think is the reason of his popularity. Then comes the secretary—Gorbunov. He was elected this year to the Academy specially to fill this post. Between the 90 members of the Academy, the average age of whom is 65 years, it was impossible to find an active enough member to do the secretarial work.

He is not much of a scientist; in the recent years he done some expeditions in the South East of Russia, very daring ones. So he is rather an explorer. Probably he is the only person on the Council who has some personality. In any case when you talk to him, he does express views and opinions, what others scarcely dare. Then comes our friend B.[15] Do you remember a short man with a small beard that I once brought to college. He is a peculiar mixture of a journalist, economist and philosopher. He is all right, but terribly frightened of me now, and avoids seeing me. The next one is a chemist B.[16] A technical chemist, supposed to be shrewd, but no more. It is difficult to say much about him; he is kind and noncommittal in conversation. Probably a very suitable member of the Council; fills the space and does not disturb anyone.

Finally one comes to a physicist Vavilov;[17] he is young, only 45. I doubt if you know him by name, his work was in the fluorescence of liquids. You know the sort of work when you pass a beam of light through a vessel filled with liquid and observe the light perpendicularly. Once installed the apparatus you can play for all your life, changing the liquids, the number of which is immense, and you can also vary the spectra of the primary beam. And thus you have such a number of combinations that it can keep a research student busy all his life and give him the feeling of satisfaction that he is doing scientific work. He never did nothing else.

I was always surprised, why Vavilov got into the Academy, when even with our poor stock of physicists we have such people as Skobeltzine,[18] Fock[19] and others, which are miles better than Vavilov.[20] I think you will find the secret in that Vavilov is a very polished man, who knows what to say and when to say it; that pleases everybody.

In general I regret so much that I am not a polished man, as this would make my life so much easier. But I know a great scientist, who without any

15. Probably Nikolai Bukharin.
16. Probably A. A. Baikov, a metallurgist.
17. S. I. Vavilov, who was president of the academy, 1945–51. He was the brother of N. I. Vavilov, Lysenko's chief opponent.
18. D. V. Skobeltzine, who was elected an academician in 1946.
19. V. A. Fock, who was elected an academician in 1939.
20. In view of this attitude it is ironic that Kapitza's Institute was renamed after Vavilov, following the latter's death.

well-polished manners, got as far as only you can get. But this is in England, where there are too many people with good manners and their value is not too great. It appears that here they value good manners much more as they are not so common.

Now the last member of the Council is Frumkin, the physical-chemist. He is the only man on the Council with scientific standing. If he is not too brilliant, he is shrewd and honest and devoted to science. He is a melancholic looking man, never gets excited, is cynical in his attitude. He was kind to me and was never frightened of keeping in touch with me during all the period of my detention. So I have a feeling of deep appreciation of his personality.

Well this is the Council of the Academy of Sciences, as you see a not very attractive picture. I think the R.S.[21] at its worst never had such a collection of specimens in its Council.

They never take any interest, whatsoever, in my Institute, not a single member of the Council has visited me, never a word of sympathy or interest. I feel myself pretty indifferent towards them too. At present I had only two collisions with them and both times I managed to get what I wanted, and they know by now that I am not a lamb.

The other scientists are also quite indifferent to me. My former teacher Joffé ignored me all this time, and only now suddenly burst out in kindness. He is the head of the physical group of the Academy, and is the leader in physics in general. As I have no desire to take part in his doings, I keep apart and out. So you see how lonely I am.

All my hopes are in the young people, which I want to pick out from the university undergraduates. I give a course of lectures there, to make friendship with them and get them interested in my work.

You see in my loneliness how much I do appreciate any signs of friendship from Cambridge scientists, and I hope to start corresponding with them. But still more I shall be glad if my friends will come to visit "the man behind the bars."

Now all my desire is to resume work as soon as possible and to do the experiments with the magnetic field and [helium] which have been interrupted. I hope this will take three or four years, and what will happen next I do not anticipate. But my actions are determined and I do not scatter my energy beside my scientific work. I agree with you by 100% that I must "keep my nose to the grind stone." Your excellent advice. But now do you see why I am so anxious to get my apparatus as soon as possible? Sooner I could get, sooner I could start my work. And then I am sure my state of mind will get

21. Royal Society of London.

more balanced, and I am sure that then all these old idiots of the Academy of Sciences will stop to irritate me as much as they do now.

Things with the Lab. do not go so badly, even if it is impossible to do as many things as well as in the Mond. Considering the comforts of the work these are all small things. I have now a new assistant director, a lady engineer, very experienced and good. She is a most excellent worker and with her help (she is helping me very well), by the end of March the lab will be ready for the installation of my Cambridge apparatus. The greatest difficulty which I encounter is the supply of small articles, even if they are manufactured here. And now I shall explain you why this is so.

You see Soviet industry is growing at a terrific rate and all is done to make its growing organised and well planned, so that all the system of supply and production is also well planned and organised. But the supply of the factory, which is operating according to a definite plan, must be anticipated in details at the beginning of the year, and evidently represents its demands in very large figures. Such a system is indeed quite unsuitable for the supply of laboratories. I have written and spoken to the authorities that the labs must be supplied in a different way, and I think that the people here begin to recognise that the system of supply must be altered for the scientific institutions. But, at present, if for instance we require four bars of phosphore bronze, the need of which we had not anticipated in the beginning of the year, we must get it as an exception and the permission of the sub-secretary of the Heavy Industries is required and this means a lot of correspondence, which is equally extensive do we require 10 kilograms, 10 tons or 10 loads of stuff. And so even if the Institute is given sufficient money, and even if the industries are quite decent, we are actually very badly supplied.

Indeed all this is temporary. In two, three years time all will change, but before it is changed we must live and work. And you know how slowly a bureaucratic government machine moves and changes, specially now when all the interests are to see the industries growing and the interest in science is very academic. As to get the different supplies from abroad the bother is about the same. We are given quite sufficient of the foreign exchange, but to get anything, again you had to make a plan at the beginning of the year. And then all that you ask must pass through a certain controlling organisation, which must satisfy itself that the given article is not procurable in the Union, competitive tenders are asked, etc. And all this applies to the small articles as well as to the big ones. You may well imagine what an amount of writing we must do and what a terrific stock of people we must keep to carry through all this bureaucratic work. I dare say all this will be eventually changed, but at the moment you see how immensely helpful you are in sending me all sorts of small supplies of general articles. And this is the reason of difficulties of which you express surprise in your letter.

I know that you run your laboratory with great consideration to economy and to the financial welfare. And I discern in your letter a certain conflict between the fatherly attitude towards me and desiring to help, and the Director of the Cavendish Laboratory trying to keep the business end as high as possible. Let the father win! After all you must not complain, as after I left Cambridge, the Physical Department is left with a laboratory worth 25 kilo pounds equipped with the best cryogenic equipment and I reckon you will be left with a five figured reserve in capital. You will have several excellently trained people like Pearson, Laurmann, Miss Stebbing.[22] Indeed, you may say that you had spent a lot of energy in all this, and you are right. But even if you pulled the ropes I provided them! I even hoped that the Varsity and the R.S. will acknowledge my contribution and my letter of resignation, but the man behind the bars is not considerately treated. And you must not grumble if you are left with a few hundred pounds less than you anticipated. Just keep in mind my position. Absolutely alone, half chained and very miserable. All my hope in regaining some happiness is in the anticipation of starting my work, and without your help and sympathy this is impossible. And if you take a formal attitude I am done in.

I take it from Rabinovitch that you have consented in transferring any apparatus and equipment in the Mond in original or duplicate. You certainly could not have thought that making the original list by memory I have not omitted a few items which I hope may be included eventually. That I am not greedy you may see in that all that I did not need I omitted. Like the big liquid air plant (value at least £1000), the accumulators (£400), the 33 K.W. generator set (£200), the wiring (£1500), the synchronous clock you proposed to send, but in first instant I omitted as I did not think that the frequency will be normalised, but now that we introduced the standardised frequency I asked to reinclude them, besides the pendulum seconds clock. And now from all that I said you may appreciate why I am so keen to get all sorts of materials and supplies even more extensive than we had them usually in the Mond. There we had the possibility at any moment to get all we needed from the shops, and here you are, generally speaking, deprived of this possibility. Indeed I shall correspond about it all with Cockcroft and he will bring the matter before you.

Now the next point very important to me is the help of Pearson and Laurmann. Their help is indispensible to me to start and to run the lab. for the beginning, and this is why I am so keen to get them. You must not be

22. Miss Stebbing was the laboratory secretary.

afraid that I shall keep them, as much as I desire it, by the simple reason that I cannot provide the means which will induce them to stay here permanently. For the assistants and scientists are very badly paid here. Myself for instance, I get even at par, only half of what I used to get in Cambridge, and in reality actually 1/6 of my Cambridge means. But to live modestly I do not need more and never had complained of my pay. Provided I get the facilities to work, this is all I need at the moment.

To get out of this difficulty my colleagues the scientists take a number of jobs, 5-6, and in this way they manage to get quite a lot of money. I resent this way of living as it will dissipate my energy and I will be unable to do research work. I am glad Anna shares my views and we are prepared to have a modest existence. Anna was wise to bring from England plenty of clothes as all our salary goes into food. I hope that perhaps in future things may change and I shall not be forced to dissipate my energy.

But you will easily see that it will be impossible for me to expect Laurmann and Pearson to stay here longer than it is possible for me to compensate them by their normal salary to keep their families in Cambridge.

As regards the time of their arrival, I think they must follow the liquefier as soon as it is ready and sent off. I understand April the 1st is the most probable date, so about this time I suggest they should leave Cambridge. Should you like me to write officially to the Mond Committee I will do it. Let them better come together, then Laurmann can help Pearson with the language.

Now about John,[23] I am very touched in the way he acted and highly appreciate his help. Unfortunately, I cannot see how I could compensate him for his work in England, but I am sure that you will see that he gets adequately compensated. But when John comes here I will do all my possible to see that he gets a good time and something like a free trip to Caucasus or Crimea. But you know that I have plenty of sense of gratitude in my heart.

Now I have written you a long letter, and I hope this will draw a picture of my life and position which are far from enviable. I also hope that I can reckon on your sympathy and support, and I know I shall get it, as you always were good to me, and especially now that I so badly require it. In my impatience to get to work I try to hurry you, and you must not get angry as it is only natural. You would not expect me to ask you to delay the work on the liquefier? Would you? Then everything is O.K.

Now I wrote a long letter to you, and should you like it I shall proceed in doing so. To talk to you is a great pleasure to me and I hope you would not mind.

---

23. John Cockcroft, who supervised sending Kapitza his apparatus.

Meanwhile my most kind regards to you and to Lady Rutherford. I am sending you an "ex libris" which was done here for me; you can see that the tenderness for the crocodile has not changed.

Affectionately yours,

Peter Kapitza.

P.S. Anna has retyped my letter to make the reading possible, and to correct to some extent my spelling.

Rutherford responded sympathetically, although he chided Kapitza that he expected anytime to receive a request for the paint from the walls of the Mond.[24] But again he insisted that the harder Kapitza worked, the less time he would have for other troubles. And to emphasize the wisdom of his view with the profundity of a proverb, he added: "A reasonable number of fleas is good for a dog—but I expect you feel you have more than the average number!"[25]

Despite having few friends in Moscow—most people were afraid to associate with him—Kapitza settled down to a more agreeable routine by the spring of 1936. Though prices were quite high, food was abundant, especially such delicacies as oysters, caviar, and smoked sturgeon, which would make even the Trinity College "gourmands at the high table dribble."[26] The Academy of Sciences gave him a satisfactory flat and he could look forward to living in the director's home on the grounds of the Institute for Physical Problems. The institute itself, magnificently situated among parks on the side of a hill overlooking Moscow, was nearing completion, and his incompetent chief assistant, over whom he had no authority, had been replaced. Laurmann and Pearson came that summer and, with visits back to Cambridge, for their freedom had been an issue of serious university concern, each remained in Moscow a few years. Kapitza, thus, slowly built up the physical plant and the research program of his new laboratory. After a year of inactivity and isolation, and another year spent acquiring his material resources, Kapitza was back to work in late 1936. The timing was fortunate, for Rutherford, upon whom he depended so much for aid and encouragement, died in October 1937.

24. Rutherford letter to Kapitza, 23 Mar. 1936.
25. Rutherford letter to Kapitza, 15 May 1936.
26. Kapitza letter to Rutherford, 26 Apr. 1936.

≪ 6 ≫

Epilogue

The Institute for Physical Problems of the Academy of Sciences of the USSR, under Kapitza's direction, became one of the major research institutions in Russia. In the Soviet view, this justified the wisdom of commandeering his talents. Kapitza, in fact, was extremely fortunate, for to complement his experimental skills he was joined in 1937 by the brilliant young mathematical physicist, Lev Landau. Kapitza's pioneering work in the superfluidity and superconductivity of liquid helium at temperatures near absolute zero, recognized by the Nobel Prize in 1978, therefore received theoretical explanation, an accomplishment for which Landau won the Nobel Prize also, some years earlier, in 1962. Another significant contribution of the institute, which marked it as an active center of science, was the now-classic encyclopedic series of monographs on theoretical physics written by Landau and another talented member of Kapitza's group, Yevgeny Lifshitz. Kapitza, thus, was wrong in the fear he expressed in his letter of 5 June 1935, that he would not be able to influence the rise of science in Russia. The question of "confidence" seems also to have resolved itself in time.

But not all was rosy, for gathering war clouds and Kapitza's independent spirit presented occasions for anxiety. Many details of his life after 1934 are known only sketchily, for the information that emerges from the Soviet Union is fragmentary at best, and often contradictory. Landau, it seems, was jailed in 1938 as a German spy. In ill health and after a year in prison, he was released only after Kapitza, said to be Stalin's chief scientific adviser, protested personally and threatened to refuse to work.[1] Regardless of Soviet need for

1. Obituary notice of Landau, *New York Times*, 3 Apr. 1968.

Kapitza's talents, such action was a severe challenge to authority and underscores the intensity of his moral feelings. It is pure speculation to wonder how close he himself came to being incarcerated on this occasion or at other times, in the type of prison camp described, for example, in Anatoly Marchenko's *My Testimony*, or the more sophisticated "research institute" of the postwar years, depicted in Alexander Solzhenitsyn's *First Circle*.

During World War II Kapitza appears to have been concerned mainly with the liquefaction of oxygen for the steel industry and after the war with microwave electronics, an offshoot of his interest in electrical power transmission.[2] Yet, although the view is widely contradicted by his colleagues in the West, various sources credit Kapitza with supervision of the laboratories for development of atomic bombs, hydrogen bombs, and strategic uses of cosmic ray energy.[3] Support is lent to this interpretation of his activities by his mysterious absence as Director of the Institute for Physical Problems between 1946 and 1955, after which date he regained this position. But this can be, and has been, oppositely interpreted as a period in which he was out of favor for his independent attitudes and for having pursued some unsuccessful lines of work during the war, and it can be seen as evidence that he was "rehabilitated" only after Stalin's death in 1953. It is even claimed that he lost his post for refusing to be involved with nuclear weapons,[4] though, if true, the Soviet project under I. V. Kurchatov seems not to have been delayed as a result. Kapitza himself has denied working in either nuclear physics or its applications, despite contrary reports in the foreign press.[5]

2. Sir John Cockcroft, quoted in V. K. McElheny, "Kapitza to visit England," *Science*, 152 (6 May 1966), 744.

3. *Who's Who in U.S.S.R., 1965/66;* J. Alvin Kugelmass and Jack Goulden, "The double cross that gave the Reds the H-BOMB," *Look*, 18 (13 July 1954), 24–27; A. M. Biew, *Kapitsa. The Story of the British-Trained Scientist Who Invented the Russian Hydrogen Bomb* (London: Frederick Muller, 1956).

4. *The Observer*, 3 Apr. 1966. See Herbert York, *The Advisors: Oppenheimer, Teller, and the Superbomb* (San Francisco: W. H. Freeman, 1976), pp. 37–40, for the most likely explanation of Kapitza's period of official disgrace: he argued with secret police boss and overall head of nuclear weapons work, Lavrenti Beria, about the role his institute could best play in this task. Also see Strobe Talbott, ed., *Khrushchev Remembers. The Last Testament* (New York: Bantam, 1976), pp. 67–73.

5. D. ter Haar, ed., *The Collected Papers of P. L. Kapitza* (Oxford: Pergamon, 1967), vol. 3, p. 154.

An American reviewer of a volume of Kapitza's essays has compared him, with some justification it seems, to J. Robert Oppenheimer:

> Both were developers of leading schools of physics in their respective nations, to which they returned (albeit in different circumstances) from European centers of learning. Both were distinguished organizers in fostering the growth of modern physics in their countries. Recognizing the importance of big facilities in the future of experimental science, both were closely associated with the development of "big physics" in their respective countries. Both were driving forces during the Second World War in their countries' wartime science efforts. Both suffered precipitous falls from grace when they refused to give way to hysterias of the political moment that were running rampant in their countries; and both were eventually vindicated and enjoyed rehabilitation as heroes. As articulate, culture scientists and statesmen of science, both have deeply and eloquently expressed their concerns for humanity's survival in a nuclear age.[6]

Kapitza's forthright personality involved him in several other controversial issues within Russia. He signed a petition protesting any "rehabilitation" of Stalin, after Khrushchev's famous denunciation of the despot in 1956, before the Twentieth Congress of the Communist Party of the Soviet Union. In 1962 Kapitza also publicly condemned the misapplication of Marxist dialectics to judge the truth of scientific discoveries, citing the harm done to Soviet science by former opposition to Linus Pauling's theory of chemical bonding, Werner Heisenberg's concept of the uncertainty principle, cybernetics, and ideas in biology that differed from those of Lysenko. More recently, he was outspoken in criticizing plans to construct a large paper mill and cellulose plant complex on the shores of Lake Baikal, contending that the deep Siberian lake would be polluted.[7] In 1973 his name was conspicuously absent from the list of academicians who condemned one of their fellows, Andrei Sakharov, for his outspoken defense of human rights in the Soviet Union. No doubt Kapitza was acutely conscious of the analogy between Sakharov's troubles with the Kremlin and his own difficulties in 1934–35, although

---

6. Sidney D. Drell, review of ibid., in *Science*, 161 (2 Aug. 1968), 456.

7. V. K. McElheny, "Kapitza's visit to England," *Science*, 153 (12 Aug. 1966), 725–27. See also McElheny (n. 2).

the success of the international scientific effort to aid Sakharov in 1973 indicated how much the science–government relationship had matured.[8] Kapitza's plan to confine himself only to pure science and avoid "social" work, thus, was abandoned, as might have been predicted with such an outspoken individual.

Many honors came to Kapitza, from abroad as well as his own country. He was elected to full membership in the Academy of Sciences of the USSR in 1939, and later to foreign membership in the national academies of Sweden and the United States. During the Stalin era he received three Orders of Lenin, the Moscow Defense Medal, and a Hero of Socialist Labor award, while after his resumption of normal activities he was given the Order of the Red Banner of Labor and yet another Order of Lenin. Kapitza also received numerous scientific awards, perhaps the most appreciated being the Rutherford Medal of the British Institute of Physics and the Physical Society in 1966. By this time his government permitted him to travel abroad and his visit to England was a sentimental homecoming. He delivered a lecture of Rutherford reminiscences to the Royal Society, whose president, Baron Patrick Blackett, was a colleague from the Cavendish days. In Cambridge his host was Sir John Cockcroft, Master of the newly built Churchill College. And he dined in Trinity College, where he suddenly realized that, unlike the other Fellows, he was not wearing a black gown. When he asked if he might borrow one, a waiter asked when he had last dined at High Table. "Thirty-two years," replied Kapitza. "Just a moment, Sir," said the waiter, who quickly returned with not any old gown, but Kapitza's own.[9]

Kapitza had long had an interest in science education, going out of his way in the 1930s to give courses at Moscow University in order to meet young people, for the research institutes of the Soviet Academy of Sciences are not considered teaching establishments also, while the universities conduct relatively little research. In his frequent speeches in England, he described the Russian efforts to select and train science students, seeing great hopes for the future in youth. As an elder statesman of science and as a Pugwash participant in conferences on world disarmament, he also commented sadly:

8. *Science*, 182 (20 Oct. 1973), 334.
9. "Carry on Jeeveski," *The Guardian*, 5 May 1966.

The year that Rutherford died there disappeared forever the happy days of free scientific work which gave us such delight in our youth. Science has lost her freedom. Science has become a productive force. She has become rich but she has become enslaved and part of her is veiled in secrecy. I do not know whether Rutherford would continue nowadays to joke and laugh as he used to do.[10]

By his successful efforts to establish a flourishing research school and by his uncompromising insistence on the moral conditions necessary for creative work, Kapitza may be credited substantially for the current eminence of Soviet science. Despite Kapitza's unwillingness, his career brought science and government appreciably closer together, and, for good or ill, this has been the direction in the twentieth century. It is the beginnings of this ambivalence, the difficulty of securing unalloyed happiness or righteousness, that we find on a personal scale in Kapitza's story and especially in his letter to Rutherford of 20 October 1935:

My dear Professor,

Life is an incomprehensible thing. We have difficulties in clearing up single physical phenomena, so I suppose humanity will never disentangle the fate of a human being, specially as complicated as my own. It is such a complexity of all sorts of phenomena that it is better not to question its logical coherence. After all we are only small particles of floating matter in a stream which we call fate. All that we can manage is to deflect slightly our track and keep afloat. The stream governs us.

The stream carrying a Russian is fresh, vigorous, even fascinating, and consequently rough. It is wonderfully suited for a reconstructer, economist, but is it suited for a scientist like me? Future will show it. In any case the country earnestly looks forward to see science develop and take a prominent part in the social organisation. But all is new here and the position of science has to be newly determined. In such a condition mistakes are inevitable. We must not be too hard judges and never forget that the object is a pioneer one.

I have no ill feeling, only I am not confident in my personal strength and abilities. Indeed I will do my best to resume here the scientific work in line in which "Nature" endowed me and also help to develop science in Russia. I

10. P. L. Kapitza, "Recollections of Lord Rutherford," *Proceedings of the Royal Society,* A294 (1966), 137.

am even surprised to find that I have more force to withstand more than I ever could expect, like this year. I never dreamt that to be deprived of doing my scientific work should be for me such a trial, but now it is over, in any case the worst of it. . . .

Your most affectionate
Peter Kapitza.

≪ Appendix ≫

Petition to the Soviet government, composed in
December 1934, never circulated
"Professor Pierre Kapitza"

The undersigned scientists beg to be allowed to place before the Government of the United Soviet Socialistic Republics their views upon a matter affecting the interests of the scientific world at large.

1. We understand that when Professor Pierre Kapitza, who has been engaged upon physical investigations in the University of Cambridge during the past twelve years, was visiting Russia in the autumn of 1934 it was intimated to him by the Russian Government that he must remain in Russia and engage upon scientific work there, and accordingly he was not allowed to return to Cambridge. We are fully aware that, as a Russian subject, his Government are acting within their legal rights in detaining him in Russia and requiring him to prosecute his scientific work there. It is however in the belief that the Russian Government do not fully appreciate the issues which have been raised by this sudden action that we, as representatives of science in a number of countries, venture to approach them on the matter and place the following considerations before them from the point of view of international science.

2. Many of us have followed closely Kapitza's work at the Cavendish Laboratory since he went to Cambridge and realised that he was opening up new lines of investigation which promised great value in the study of physics and allied branches of science. We know that quite recently a new laboratory was specially built for him to enable him to perfect his investigations in the field of Magnetic Research; that the past few years have been spent by him upon a laborious programme of preparatory work; and that the full exploitation of the new plant and equipment placed at his disposal was about to begin. The keen disappointment felt by his brother physicists throughout the world will be understood when we say that it seemed to them that his work was on the eve of fruition and that they were looking forward to his achievement of great advances in the particular field of physical science to which he has devoted himself. His own feelings are a matter personal to him, but we may be permitted to point out that working as he has been in close associa-

tion with the Cavendish Laboratory the constant exchange of ideas, the sharing of a common scientific atmosphere, and the stimulus resulting from the close contact of workers in allied fields are vital to success. For him to be suddenly cut off from this environment must—if we can place ourselves in his position—be a shattering disappointment. To deny to a scientist the means of pursuing his investigations in the *milieu* most favourable to them is one of the most grievous injuries he can suffer, and through him the whole scientific world suffers too. We should also like to point out that Kapitza in Cambridge was engaged in investigations in the domain of pure science with the hope of adding to our knowledge of the magnetic properties of matter—a study of no immediate practical bearing but one of outstanding theoretical interest to scientists throughout the world. The unique methods of attack developed by Kapitza gave promise of adding much to our knowledge in this difficult field.

3. There is one other international aspect of the matter to which we must refer. It is a truism to say that to-day science has no national frontiers. Scientists throughout the world are more conscious than they have ever been that they cannot do effective work in isolation but are members of a single team pushing forward the frontiers of knowledge. There has therefore grown up a practice of the utmost freedom of exchange of scientific ideas and laboratory facilities between different nations. England, like other countries, has to our knowledge welcomed young scientific workers from all over the world and has freely offered them opportunity to pursue their researches. This exchange of facilities, this give-and-take, is a vital principle of modern scientific work, and any threat to that principle engages the alarm of the scientific world as a whole. We are seriously apprehensive of the damage likely to be done to international science by an incident of this kind, resulting as it has in the sudden interruption of scientific investigations which have involved lengthy preparation and which were being undertaken in a University, where, as many of us can testify, the door has always been kept open to scientific workers irrespective of their race, nationality or politics. We should like to add that the facilities so freely afforded by the Royal Society and the University of Cambridge to Kapitza to enable him to carry out his work under the best conditions seem to us an admirable example of that type of international scientific co-operation which many of us would like to see extended. The work being done by Kapitza in Cambridge has not only added materially to the scientific knowledge of the world, but has at the same time enhanced the already high reputation of Russian science.

4. We therefore respectfully request that the Russian Government should re-examine the situation in the light of the repercussions which their present decision is likely to have upon the interests of international scientific co-

operation, and we beg to assure them that if they found themselves able to alter that decision their action would find a warm response among Kapitza's scientific colleagues in many countries.

Rutherford letter to *The Times*, 29 April 1935
"Professor Kapitza. Retention in Russia Shock to the Scientific World"

The news of the retention in Russia of Professor P. Kapitza, F.R.S., Director of the Royal Society Mond Laboratory in Cambridge, came as a severe shock to the scientific world, and, quite apart from the general problem of the liberty of the individual, has raised some questions of vital importance with regard to international scientific relations.

Professor Kapitza has been working in Cambridge for the past 12 years on problems of pure science, and since 1923 has been financed from British sources. His marked originality of mind and technical abilities so strongly impressed his colleagues that a handsome donation was made by the Royal Society in order to construct and equip a new laboratory in Cambridge to allow him to continue his researches under the most favourable conditions. At the same time the Royal Society appointed him to one of its few professorships. The new laboratory was formally opened three years ago by Mr. Baldwin as Chancellor of the University.

The laboratory is provided with special apparatus for the study of magnetic properties of matter in intense magnetic fields at the lowest possible temperatures. Kapitza had devised a new method of obtaining a magnetic field stronger than had ever been obtained before, and also a new and simple type of helium liquefier for the production of liquid helium in quantity at a relatively low cost. Liquid helium is invaluable in the laboratory as the only method of producing the lowest possible temperatures. Everything was ready to combine the use of these two techniques developed by Kapitza in order to study the properties of matter near the absolute zero under the influence of intense magnetic fields. It was confidently expected by the scientific world that these new experiments would yield results which would add markedly to our knowledge of the structure of matter.

Last summer Professor Kapitza visited Russia as in previous years, gave some lectures there, and was invited to attend the conference in honour of the great Russian chemist, Mendeleef. A few days before his return to Cambridge he was officially informed that he must stay and work in Russia. Professor Kapitza, although he had long resided in England, remained a Soviet citizen (and a loyal one who regularly visited Russia). By the distinction of his work here, which added materially to the already high reputation of Russian science, he was influential in promoting happy scientific relations between the two countries and in securing for his scientific compatriots a cordial welcome in English laboratories.

While no one disputes that the Soviet authorities have a legal claim upon Professor Kapitza's services, their sudden action in commandeering them without any previous warning has profoundly disturbed the University and the scientific world. He was not even allowed to return to discuss with the University authorities and the Royal Society arrangements for carrying on the work of the laboratory of which he is director. It requires no imagination to realize how painful Professor Kapitza's own position is, for he was on the eve of completing the experiments in Cambridge for which he had so long prepared, and from which he had reason to expect so much new light on the properties of matter. Scientific men have watched with admiration the rapid advance of science in Russia, but even under ideal conditions it would require much time to reconstruct in Russia the unique equipment specially constructed by Professor Kapitza in Cambridge. Science is international and every scientist hopes that it will long remain so, and the facilities granted to Professor Kapitza in this country are a good example of this fact. Apart from the personal factor, it may matter little in the long run whether the investigations which Kapitza had in view are ultimately made in Russia or in this country, though it is important to avoid waste of time and effort in duplicating costly apparatus which is already available and has taken so many years and so much planning to prepare. But the personal factor is a vital one in creative work. It is inevitable that Professor Kapitza has been greatly disturbed by this sudden frustration of his work and by the conflict of loyalties involved in the action of the Soviet Government, and reports from Russia made it clear that his health has been seriously impaired by anxiety and disappointment. Men of scientific originality and imagination like Kapitza require an atmosphere of complete mental tranquillity in which to do their creative work. It would be a great misfortune in the interests of science in the world at large if, through lack of sympathy or understanding, conditions should arise which would inhibit Kapitza from giving his best to the world.

It is to be feared that while the Soviet Government has acted within its legal rights, and no doubt with the best intentions, there has been a lack of appreciation of the effects of its sudden action. May we hope that the Soviet Government, which has given so many proofs of its interest in the development of science, will pursue a generous and long-sighted policy, and will see its way to meet the wishes of scientific men, not only of this country, but throughout the world, by enabling Kapitza to choose the environment in which he can most effectively utilize the special creative gifts with which he is endowed? It would be a tragedy if these gifts were rendered sterile by failure to grasp the psychological situation.

F. Gowland Hopkins letter to *The Times*, 1 May 1935
"Professor Kapitza"

All in this country who are concerned with the progress of science, and the many who would deeply regret any further suspension of the exceedingly important and disinterested researches of Professor Kapitza, will wish to support Lord Rutherford's reasoned and powerful appeal to the Soviet Government which appears in your issue of to-day. His letter makes the issues abundantly clear, but you will perhaps allow me to add a few words from the special standpoint of the Royal Society.

The circumstances that the provision of a large sum for the erection of the Mond Laboratory at Cambridge, intended for the housing of Professor Kapitza's labours, made a serious inroad into the research funds of the society, together with the further circumstance that he is one of its few research professors, might be viewed as minor factors in the situation were not these endowments derived from trust funds. As trustee for the estates of generous testators whose sole aim was the advancement of knowledge, the society cannot fail to be disturbed when the benefits accruing from their generosity are held in abeyance. The present situation entitles it, I think, to some sympathy.

The Royal Society fully recognizes the legal claim of the Soviet authorities upon Professor Kapitza's services, but ventures to believe that with full understanding of the position they would wish those services to be rendered wherever they can best promote the interests of pure and disinterested science as an international pursuit. The society is supported in this belief by its knowledge of the generous support that pure science, no less than its application, is receiving at the hands of the Soviet Government.

Lord Rutherford's letter has made abundantly clear the importance of Kapitza's work, its disinterested nature, and the reasons why, for the present at least, it should be continued at Cambridge.

The country of Pavlov later this year is to extend generous hospitality to an International Congress of Physiologists. It would be a happy circumstance, in particular for its British visitors, if the Government of that country could just now further recognize the internationalism of science by allowing labours so well begun to continue where they can most rapidly progress.

Henry E. Armstrong letter to *The Times*, 7 May 1935
"Foreign Scientists in Britain. Professor Kapitza's Recall to Russia"

I venture to think that my young colleagues, Lord Rutherford and Sir Frederick Gowland Hopkins, are putting a "severe gloss" upon the loss to Cambridge of Professor Kapitza. Fairly in touch as I am with matters scientific, I fail to see any signs of "severe shock to the scientific world" such as

Lord Rutherford describes; rather is there a feeling of relief, at least among our younger men, to judge from my correspondence. I am even urged to give expression to this.

My right to intervene must rest upon my being the senior Fellow of the Royal Society, if not the senior opinion among academic workers generally. Little short of 60 years old in the Royal Society, it is 70 years this spring since I began my scientific career. I therefore have seen much happen—two great German wars and a multitude of smaller ones. I also have Russian sympathies, having from my student days had many Russian friends, among them the intellectual giant Mendeleef; I am also privileged to be a member of the Russian Academy of Sciences, now the Soviet Academy.

When I began we had no school of chemistry of account under English control; that I entered was in charge of a German, the great Hofmann, who left us in 1865, in despair of ever making chemists of us. Throughout the country most of our chemical work was in German hands; what little we did was too often published in German journals. I was educated mainly at a German university and can never repay the debt I owe to its training. Still, on my return I was one of several who made up their minds that they would develop chemistry as an English subject; foundations were laid up to the War and we have now raised ourselves at least to equality with the world—we no longer need foreign help.

A year or two ago I protested in *Nature* against the importation by Manchester of a physical chemist from somewhere in the Balkans. I did so on no personal grounds, simply because Manchester—to use a vulgarism—had sniffed at the English candidates as not good enough. How are we to make progress if we do not employ those we train? At Cambridge and elsewhere men are hugging chains, eating their hearts out for lack of opportunity to develop their talent under practical conditions. Why, then, should we import foreign labour?

Surely Cambridge has put too high a value upon Professor Kapitza? Some of us fail to see that proof has been given of his genius. Apparently he is a clever mechanic. He has made certain minor improvements in the apparatus for liquefying helium. He was constructing a magnet of great power. We are a mechanical race, if we are anything. Surely there are hosts of young men who could do the work? Cambridge teaching cannot be of much avail if, among Faraday's countrymen, men cannot be found able to undertake the construction of magnets on any scale that may be needed. What, too, of the importance of the work—is not relatively too much importance being attached to the doings of the atom-smashing brigade led by Lord Rutherford? Could we not well afford to send them out into the Sahara and await their return, say, 10 years hence, with results of real significance? Do not our national needs demand work of a very different type—what is the use, for example, of atom-smashing when cattle are being slaughtered in thousands upon thousands because we know nothing of foot-and-mouth disease?

Sir F. Gowland Hopkins refers to inroads made upon Royal Society funds in support of Professor Kapitza. Not a few of us think that this special use of the Mond fund is unjustifiable. I have little doubt that my old friend Dr. Ludwig Mond would not have been in favour of such an expenditure—his money was little short of earmarked for application to the maintenance of the International Catalogue of Scientific Literature, which the Society has tragically allowed to lapse. I am also sure that my life-long friend Messel would have objected to his money being devoted to an academic professorship. The whole policy of the Society in founding research professorships, of an ultra-academic type, is suspect. Lord Rutherford speaks of Professor Kapitza as subject to Soviet authority—which can only mean that he is still a Russian. Why, then, was he made a Fellow of the Royal Society?

We are living in a strange world. Germany, once the home of a high intellectuality, is now almost persecuting those who would pursue knowledge. Russia, sometimes thought of as barbaric in its outlook, is advisedly setting out to order national development, through systematic application of scientific method. In so doing it is setting a great example to the world. We have no such enlightened outlook—we make but sporadic use of our knowledge and have no special care for the men who might apply it, if calculated opportunity were given to them. Surely the Russians are right? They are said to lack mechanical skill. If a paragon of mechanical ability be advertised as living abroad, they cannot logically do otherwise than recall him. Instead of leading a lotus life at Cambridge, he, too, may well be doing national work of a far higher order than even that involved in magnetizing atoms to destruction.

⧼⧼ Index ⧽⧽